D0095101

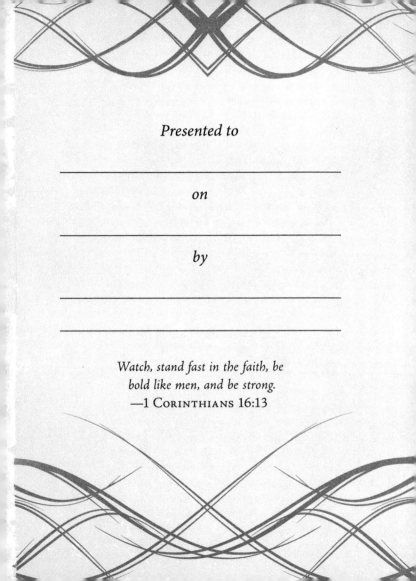

Presented to

_____

on

_____

by

_____

_____

Watch, stand fast in the faith, be bold like men, and be strong.
—1 CORINTHIANS 16:13

SPIRIT*LED* PROMISES *FOR*

MEN

PASSIO
THE ART OF AUTHENTIC FAITH

MODERN
ENGLISH
VERSION

Most CHARISMA HOUSE BOOK GROUP products are available at special quantity discounts for bulk purchase for sales promotions, premiums, fund-raising, and educational needs. For details, write Charisma House Book Group, 600 Rinehart Road, Lake Mary, Florida 32746, or telephone (407) 333-0600.

SpiritLed Promises for Men
Published by Passio
Charisma Media/Charisma House Book Group
600 Rinehart Road
Lake Mary, Florida 32746
www.charismahouse.com

This book or parts thereof may not be reproduced in any form, stored in a retrieval system, or transmitted in any form by any means—electronic, mechanical, photocopy, recording, or otherwise—without prior written permission of the publisher, except as provided by United States of America copyright law.

Scripture taken from the Holy Bible, Modern English Version, copyright © 2014 by Military Bible Association. All rights reserved. Used by permission.

Copyright © 2015 by Passio
All rights reserved

Cover design by Lisa Rae McClure
Design Director: Justin Evans

Library of Congress Control Number: 2014960253
International Standard Book Number: 978-1-62998-226-7
E-book ISBN: 978-1-62998-249-6

First edition

15 16 17 18 19 — 987654321
Printed in the United States of America

God is looking for broken men who have judged themselves in the light of the cross of Christ. When He wants anything done, He takes up men who have come to the end of themselves, whose confidence is not in themselves, but in God.

—H. A. IRONSIDE

CONTENTS

INTRODUCTION

*A man may lose the good things of this life
against his will; but if he loses the eternal blessings, he does so with his own consent.*
—AUGUSTINE

*God loves with a great love the man whose heart
is bursting with a passion for the impossible.*
—WILLIAM BOOTH

WHAT DOES IT mean to be a man after God's heart?
To know what a true man is you need look no fur-
ther than the life of Jesus Christ. It means your life is in
harmony with the Father. What is important to Him is
important to you. What burdens Him burdens you. It
takes enormous courage to follow God's leading in the
Christian life. Some of His callings demand the best that
you can summon. Some of life's tests stretch you to the
limit. Spiritual courage is a character quality every man
must develop stronger. That strength can be found in
God's promises.

God desires that you bond with Him. When you are
convinced He has your best interests at heart, you won't
question where He is leading you. At times the path

may seem narrow, but it is never crooked. God's way is always clear and direct. By meditating on and applying God's promises you'll learn to nurture a life of faith and Christian growth as you prepare for what He has called you to. When you apply His promises to the issues of life that bring challenge or questions, you'll experience His promises replenishing your deepest felt needs with the strength and assurance you long for.

SpiritLed Promises for Men will nourish and replenish your heart, mind, and soul. You'll experience your spirit being bolstered with comforting scriptures from God's Word. These are specially selected promises for two hundred important life topics that renew your strength, hope, comfort, and confidence for everything that life delivers. Apply each scripture personally, and you'll experience the power of God's Word in action. You'll realize the joy in celebrating victories in many areas of your life when you learn to trust God to meet your every need.

God wants us all to experience a deeper walk with Him. He wants men to become secure enough to confront fear, to take risks, and make commitments. The times demand big men. Men who have big hearts. Men with vision. Men whose eyes are on the far horizon and committed to a life of integrity rooted in the teachings and principles found throughout God's Word.

SpiritLed Promises for Men reveals the heart of the eternal God, and every promise is personal to you. By spending just a few minutes during the quiet times of your day, you'll find that God still speaks anew through the words of the Bible today—even through verses you've read many times before. It will open your eyes to the truth in a way that frees you from things that pull you down, such as jealousy, anger, hurt, and strife. Allow God's promises to plant seeds of hope with you that grow into what the Bible calls the fruit of the Spirit—love, joy, peace, patience, kindness, goodness, faithfulness, gentleness, and self-control. As you read you'll discover how frequently a promise from the Scriptures can offer insight and answers that turn a situation around in an instant. These promises can bring key insights and develop the strength you need to reach out to your family.

Most of the time trusting God involves placing a situation in His hands, believing He will either change it or give you what you need to endure it. God is faithful and will never let you down. He is there for you today, tomorrow, and all the days that follow. God has promised to keep you mindful of His words, but for Him to remind you, you need to know what He has said. What are you trusting God for right now? Take whatever it —is—no matter how big or how small, possible or impossible—and place it in God's capable hands. Rely on His promises to see you through to victory.

Out of one hundred men, one will read the Bible, the other ninety-nine will read the Christian.

—D. L. MOODY

ABUNDANCE

But the meek will inherit the earth, and will delight themselves in the abundance of peace.

—Psalm 37:11

A good man out of the good treasure of his heart bears what is good, and an evil man out of the evil treasure of his heart bears what is evil. For of the abundance of the heart his mouth speaks.

—Luke 6:45

Now may the God of hope fill you with all joy and peace in believing, so that you may abound in hope, through the power of the Holy Spirit.

—Romans 15:13

Now to Him who is able to do exceedingly abundantly beyond all that we ask or imagine, according to the power that works in us.

—Ephesians 3:20

Every good gift and every perfect gift is from above and comes down from the Father of lights, with whom is no change or shadow of turning.

—James 1:17

ACCOUNTABILITY

Iron sharpens iron, so a man sharpens the countenance of his friend.

—Proverbs 27:17

But I say to you that for every idle word that men speak, they will give an account on the Day of Judgment. For by your words you will be justified, and by your words you will be condemned.

—Matthew 12:36–37

He told His disciples: "There was a rich man who had a steward who was accused to the man of wasting his resources. So he called him and said, 'How is it that I hear this about you? Give an account of your stewardship, for you may no longer be steward.'"

—Luke 16:1–2

So then each of us shall give an account of himself to God.

—Romans 14:12

For we must all appear before the judgment seat of Christ, that each one may receive his recompense in the body, according to what he has done, whether it was good or bad.

—2 Corinthians 5:10

ADULTERY

You shall not commit adultery.

—Exodus 20:14

If a man commits adultery with another man's wife, even he who commits adultery with his neighbor's wife, the adulterer and the adulteress shall surely be put to death.

—Leviticus 20:10

He who covers his sins will not prosper, but whoever confesses and forsakes them will have mercy.

—Proverbs 28:13

Do you not know that the unrighteous will not inherit the kingdom of God? Do not be deceived. Neither the sexually immoral, nor idolaters, nor adulterers, nor male prostitutes, nor homosexuals, nor thieves, nor covetous, nor drunkards, nor revilers, nor extortioners will inherit the kingdom of God.

—1 Corinthians 6:9–10

Marriage is to be honored among everyone, and the bed undefiled. But God will judge the sexually immoral and adulterers.

—Hebrews 13:4

ALCOHOL

Wine is a mocker, strong drink is raging, and whoever is deceived by it is not wise.

—Proverbs 20:1

He who loves pleasure will be a poor man; he who loves wine and oil will not be rich.

—Proverbs 21:17

Do not be among winebibbers, among riotous eaters of meat; for the drunkard and the glutton will come to poverty, and drowsiness will clothe a man with rags.

—Proverbs 23:20–21

Take heed to yourselves, lest your hearts become burdened by excessiveness and drunkenness and anxieties of life, and that Day comes on you unexpectedly.

—Luke 21:34

Envy, murders, drunkenness, carousing, and the like. I warn you, as I previously warned you, that those who do such things shall not inherit the kingdom of God.

—Galatians 5:21

AMBITION

But seek first the kingdom of God and His righteousness, and all these things shall be given to you.

—Matthew 6:33

For what will it profit a man if he gains the whole world and loses his own soul? Or what shall a man give in exchange for his soul?

—Matthew 16:26

Let nothing be done out of strife or conceit, but in humility let each esteem the other better than himself.

—Philippians 2:3

Learn to be calm, and to conduct your own business, and to work with your own hands, as we commanded you, so that you may walk honestly toward those who are outsiders and that you may lack nothing.

—1 Thessalonians 4:11–12

For all that is in the world—the lust of the flesh, the lust of the eyes, and the pride of life—is not of the Father, but is of the world. The world and its desires are passing away, but the one who does the will of God lives forever.

—1 John 2:16–17

ANGER

He who is quick tempered deals foolishly, and a man of wicked devices is hated.

—Proverbs 14:17

Make no friendship with an angry man, and with a furious man you will not go, lest you learn his ways and get a snare to your soul.

—Proverbs 22:24–25

Let all bitterness, wrath, anger, outbursts, and blasphemies, with all malice, be taken away from you. And be kind one to another, tenderhearted, forgiving one another, just as God in Christ also forgave you.

—Ephesians 4:31–32

But now you must also put away all these: anger, wrath, malice, blasphemy, and filthy language out of your mouth.

—Colossians 3:8

Therefore, my beloved brothers, let every man be swift to hear, slow to speak, and slow to anger, for the anger of man does not work the righteousness of God.

—James 1:19–20

ANOINTING

And I will raise up for Myself a faithful priest; what is in My heart and in My soul he will do it. And I will build him a sure house, and it will walk before My anointed forever.

—1 Samuel 2:35

Truly, truly I say to you, he who believes in Me will do the works that I do also. And he will do greater works than these, because I am going to My Father.

—John 14:12

You lust and do not have, so you kill. You desire to have and cannot obtain. You fight and war. Yet you do not have, because you do not ask.

—James 4:2

But you have an anointing from the Holy One, and you know all things. I have written to you, not because you do not know the truth, but because you know it, and because no lie is of the truth. Who is a liar but the one who denies that Jesus is the Christ? Whoever denies the Father and the Son is the antichrist.

—1 John 2:20–22

But the anointing which you have received from Him remains in you, and you do not need anyone to teach you. For as the same anointing teaches you concerning all things, and is truth, and is no lie, and just as it has taught you, remain in Him.

—1 John 2:27

ANSWERED PRAYER

Ask and it will be given to you; seek and you will find; knock and it will be opened to you.

—Matthew 7:7

Therefore I say to you, whatever things you ask when you pray, believe that you will receive them, and you will have them.

—Mark 11:24

If you remain in Me, and My words remain in you, you will ask whatever you desire, and it shall be done for you.

—John 15:7

Confess your faults to one another and pray for one another, that you may be healed. The effective, fervent prayer of a righteous man accomplishes much.

—James 5:16

This is the confidence that we have in Him, that if we ask anything according to His will, He hears us. So if we know that He hears whatever we ask, we know that we have whatever we asked of Him.

—1 John 5:14–15

ANXIETY

Commit your way to the Lord; trust also in Him, and He will bring it to pass. He will bring forth your righteousness as the light, and your judgment as the noonday.

—Psalm 37:5–6

In the fear of the Lord is strong confidence, and His children will have a place of refuge.

—Proverbs 14:26

Why take thought about clothing? Consider the lilies of the field, how they grow: They neither work, nor do they spin. Yet I say to you that even Solomon in all his glory was not dressed like one of these. Therefore, if God so clothes the grass of the field, which today is here and tomorrow is thrown into the oven, will He not much more clothe you, O you of little faith?

—Matthew 6:28–30

Come to Me, all you who labor and are heavily burdened, and I will give you rest. Take My yoke upon you, and learn from Me. For I am meek and lowly in heart, and you will find rest for your souls.

—Matthew 11:28–29

Then He said to His disciples, "Therefore I say to you, do not be anxious for your life, what you will eat, nor for your body, what you will wear. Life is more than food, and the body is more than clothes."

—Luke 12:22–23

ASSURANCE

For I am persuaded that neither death nor life, neither angels nor principalities nor powers, neither things present nor things to come, neither height nor depth, nor any other created thing, shall be able to separate us from the love of God, which is in Christ Jesus our Lord.

—Romans 8:38–39

God is able to make all grace abound toward you, so that you, always having enough of everything, may abound to every good work.

—2 Corinthians 9:8

For these things I suffer, but I am not ashamed, for I know whom I have believed, and am persuaded that He is able to keep that which I have committed to Him until that Day.

—2 Timothy 1:12

Let us draw near with a true heart in full assurance of faith, having our hearts sprinkled to cleanse them from an evil conscience, and our bodies washed with pure water.

—Hebrews 10:22

Whoever has the Son has life, and whoever does not have the Son of God does not have life. I have written these things to you who believe in the name of the Son of God, that you may know that you have eternal life, and that you may continue to believe in the name of the Son of God.

—1 John 5:12–13

ATTITUDE

That you put off the former way of life in the old nature, which is corrupt according to the deceitful lusts, and be renewed in the spirit of your mind; and that you put on the new nature, which was created according to God in righteousness and true holiness.

—Ephesians 4:22–24

Do all things without murmuring and disputing, that you may be blameless and harmless, sons of God, without fault, in the midst of a crooked and perverse generation, in which you shine as lights in the world.

—Philippians 2:14–15

Finally, brothers, whatever things are true, whatever things are honest, whatever things are just, whatever things are pure, whatever things are lovely, whatever things are of good report, if there is any virtue, and if there is any praise, think on these things. Do those things which you have both learned and received, and heard and seen in me, and the God of peace will be with you.

—Philippians 4:8–9

Do not lie one to another, since you have put off the old nature with its deeds, and have embraced the new nature, which is renewed in knowledge after the image of Him who created it.

—Colossians 3:9–10

For the word of God is alive, and active, and sharper than any two-edged sword, piercing even to the division of soul and spirit, of joints and marrow, and able to judge the thoughts and intents of the heart.

—Hebrews 4:12

BAD HABITS

He who has a deceitful heart finds no good, and he who has a perverse tongue falls into mischief.

—Proverbs 17:20

I urge you therefore, brothers, by the mercies of God, that you present your bodies as a living sacrifice, holy, and acceptable to God, which is your reasonable service of worship. Do not be conformed to this world, but be transformed by the renewing of your mind, that you may prove what is the good and acceptable and perfect will of God.

—Romans 12:1–2

No temptation has taken you except what is common to man. God is faithful, and He will not permit you to be tempted above what you can endure, but will with the temptation also make a way to escape, that you may be able to bear it.

—1 Corinthians 10:13

Now the works of the flesh are revealed, which are these: adultery, sexual immorality, impurity, lewdness, idolatry, sorcery, hatred, strife, jealousy, rage, selfishness, dissensions, heresies, envy, murders, drunkenness, carousing, and the like. I warn you, as I previously warned you, that those who do such things shall not inherit the kingdom of God.

—Galatians 5:19–21

But avoid profane foolish babblings, for they will increase to more ungodliness.

—2 Timothy 2:16

BATTLE FOR YOUR MIND

You will keep him in perfect peace, whose mind is stayed on You, because he trusts in You.

—Isaiah 26:3

The Spirit of the Lord is upon Me, because He has anointed Me to preach the gospel to the poor; He has sent Me to heal the broken-hearted, to preach deliverance to the captives and recovery of sight to the blind, to set at liberty those who are oppressed.

—Luke 4:18

For the weapons of our warfare are not carnal, but mighty through God to the pulling down of strongholds, casting down imaginations and every high thing that exalts itself against the knowledge of God, bringing every thought into captivity to the obedience of Christ.

—2 Corinthians 10:4–5

Be anxious for nothing, but in everything, by prayer and supplication with gratitude, make your requests known to God. And the peace of God, which surpasses all understanding, will protect your hearts and minds through Christ Jesus. Finally, brothers, whatever things are true, whatever things are honest, whatever things are just, whatever things are pure, whatever things are lovely, whatever things are of good report, if there is any virtue, and if there is any praise, think on these things.

—Philippians 4:6–8

Do not let anyone deceive you in any way. For that Day will not come unless a falling away comes first, and the man of sin is revealed, the son of destruction.

—2 Thessalonians 2:3

BINDING THE ENEMY

Your right hand, O Lord, is glorious in power. Your right hand, O Lord, shatters the enemy. In the greatness of Your excellence, You overthrow those who rise up against You. You send out Your wrath; it consumes them like stubble.

—Exodus 15:6–7

"Because your heart was timid, and you humbled yourself before the Lord when you heard what I spoke against this place and against its inhabitants, that they should become a desolation and a curse, and you have torn your clothes and wept before Me, I also have heard you, declares the Lord. Therefore, I will gather you to your fathers, and you will be gathered to your grave in peace. Your eyes will not see all the evil which I am about to bring upon this place." Then they brought the king a report.

—2 Kings 22:19–20

Then they cried out to the Lord in their trouble, and He saved them out of their distress. He made the storm calm, and the sea waves were still.

—Psalm 107:28–29

Finally, my brothers, be strong in the Lord and in the power of His might. Put on the whole armor of God that you may be able to stand against the schemes of the devil.

—Ephesians 6:10–11

Be sober and watchful, because your adversary the devil walks around as a roaring lion, seeking whom he may devour.

—1 Peter 5:8

BLAME

Judge not, that you be not judged. For with what judgment you judge, you will be judged. And with the measure you use, it will be measured again for you. And why do you see the speck that is in your brother's eye, but do not consider the plank that is in your own eye? Or how will you say to your brother, "Let me pull the speck out of your eye," when a log is in your own eye? You hypocrite! First take the plank out of your own eye, and then you will see clearly to take the speck out of your brother's eye.

—Matthew 7:1–5

Not only so, but we also boast in tribulation, knowing that tribulation produces patience, patience produces character, and character produces hope. And hope does not disappoint, because the love of God is shed abroad in our hearts by the Holy Spirit who has been given to us.

—Romans 5:3–5

My brothers, count it all joy when you fall into diverse temptations, knowing that the trying of your faith develops patience. But let patience perfect its work, that you may be perfect and complete, lacking nothing.

—James 1:2–4

Blessed is the man who endures temptation, for when he is tried, he will receive the crown of life, which the Lord has promised to those who love Him.

—James 1:12

Beloved, do not be surprised at the fiery ordeal that is taking place among you to test you, as though some strange thing happened to you.

—1 Peter 4:12

BLESSINGS

Then Jabez called on the God of Israel, saying, "Oh, that You would indeed bless me and enlarge my territory, that Your hand might be with me, and that You would keep me from evil, that it may not bring me hardship!" So God granted what he asked.

—1 Chronicles 4:10

The Lord has been mindful of us; He will bless us; He will bless the house of Israel; He will bless the house of Aaron. He will bless those who fear the Lord, both the small and great ones. The LORD shall increase you more and more, you and your children.

—Psalm 115:12–14

Do not fear, for I am with you; do not be dismayed, for I am your God. I will strengthen you, I will help you, yes, I will uphold you with My righteous right hand....For I, the LORD your God, will hold your right hand, saying to you, "Do not fear; I will help you."

—Isaiah 41:10, 13

Give, and it will be given to you: Good measure, pressed down, shaken together, and running over will men give unto you. For with the measure you use, it will be measured unto you.

—Luke 6:38

For the eyes of the Lord are on the righteous, and His ears are open to their prayers; but the face of the Lord is against those who do evil.

—1 Peter 3:12

BREAKTHROUGH

No weapon that is formed against you shall prosper, and every tongue that shall rise against you in judgment, you shall condemn. This is the heritage of the servants of the LORD, and their vindication is from Me, says the LORD.

—Isaiah 54:17

Then your light shall break forth as the morning, and your healing shall spring forth quickly, and your righteousness shall go before you; the glory of the LORD shall be your reward.

—ISAIAH 58:8

Call to Me, and I will answer you, and show you great and mighty things which you do not know.

—JEREMIAH 33:3

Finally, my brothers, be strong in the Lord and in the power of His might.

—EPHESIANS 6:10

He has delivered us from the power of darkness and has transferred us into the kingdom of His dear Son.

—COLOSSIANS 1:13

You are of God, little children, and have overcome them, because He who is in you is greater than he who is in the world.

—1 JOHN 4:4

BURNOUT

See, the LORD your God has set the land before you. Go up and possess it, just as the LORD, the God of your fathers, spoke to you. Do not fear or be discouraged.

—DEUTERONOMY 1:21

But those who wait upon the Lord shall renew their strength; they shall mount up with wings as eagles, they shall run and not be weary, and they shall walk and not faint.

—Isaiah 40:31

Do not fear, for I am with you; do not be dismayed, for I am your God. I will strengthen you, I will help you, yes, I will uphold you with My righteous right hand.

—Isaiah 41:10

And let us not grow weary in doing good, for in due season we shall reap, if we do not give up.

—Galatians 6:9

But whoever keeps His word truly has the love of God perfected in him. By this we know we are in Him. Whoever says he remains in Him ought to walk as He walked.

—1 John 2:5–6

"God shall wipe away all tears from their eyes. There shall be no more death." Neither shall there be any more sorrow nor crying nor pain, for the former things have passed away.

—Revelation 21:4

BUSINESS

But you must remember the Lord your God, for it is He who gives you the ability to get wealth, so that He may establish His covenant which He swore to your fathers, as it is today.

—Deuteronomy 8:18

Whatever your hands find to do, do with your strength; for there is no work or planning or knowledge or wisdom in Sheol, the place where you are going.

—Ecclesiastes 9:10

And the Lord answered me: Write the vision, and make it plain on tablets, that he who reads it may run.

—Habakkuk 2:2

No one can serve two masters. For either he will hate the one and love the other, or else he will hold to the one and despise the other. You cannot serve God and money.

—Matthew 6:24

And whatever you do in word or deed, do all in the name of the Lord Jesus, giving thanks to God the Father through Him.

—Colossians 3:17

CHALLENGES

No man will be able to stand against you all the days of your life. As I was with Moses, I will be with you. I will not abandon you. I will not leave you.

—Joshua 1:5

My son, do not forget my teaching, but let your heart keep my commandments; for length of days and long life and peace will they add to you.

—Proverbs 3:1–2

There is nothing better for a man than to eat and drink, and find enjoyment in his labor. This also, I saw, is from the hand of God. For who can even eat or have enjoyment more so than I? For to a man who is pleasing before Him, God gives wisdom, knowledge, and joy; but to the sinner He gives the work of gathering and collecting to give him who is pleasing before God. Also this is vanity and chasing the wind.

—Ecclesiastes 2:24–26

We are troubled on every side, yet not distressed; we are perplexed, but not in despair; persecuted, but not forsaken; cast down, but not destroyed.

—2 Corinthians 4:8–9

I can do all things because of Christ who strengthens me.

—Philippians 4:13

CHANGE

Be strong and of a good courage. Fear not, nor be afraid of them, for the Lord your God, it is He who goes with you. He will not fail you, nor forsake you.

—Deuteronomy 31:6

Create in me a clean heart, O God, and renew a right spirit within me. Do not cast me away from Your presence, and do not take Your Holy Spirit from me. Restore to me the joy of Your salvation, and uphold me with Your willing spirit.

—Psalm 51:10–12

I urge you therefore, brothers, by the mercies of God, that you present your bodies as a living sacrifice, holy, and acceptable to God, which is your reasonable service of worship. Do not be conformed to this world, but be transformed by the renewing of your mind, that you may prove what is the good and acceptable and perfect will of God.

—Romans 12:1–2

Listen, I tell you a mystery: We shall not all sleep, but we shall all be changed.

—1 Corinthians 15:51

Every good gift and every perfect gift is from above and comes down from the Father of lights, with whom is no change or shadow of turning.

—James 1:17

What does it profit, my brothers, if a man says he has faith but has no works? Can faith save him? If a brother or sister is naked and lacking daily food, and one of you says to them, "Depart in peace, be warmed and filled," and yet you give them nothing that the body needs, what does it profit? So faith by itself, if it has no works, is dead.

—James 2:14–17

CHARACTER

Blessed is the man who walks not in the counsel of the ungodly, nor stands in the path of sinners, nor sits in the seat of scoffers;

but his delight is in the law of the LORD, and in His law he meditates day and night. He will be like a tree planted by the rivers of water, that brings forth its fruit in its season; its leaf will not wither, and whatever he does will prosper.

—PSALM 1:1–3

Who may ascend the hill of the LORD? Who may stand in His holy place? He who has clean hands and a pure heart; who has not lifted up his soul unto vanity, nor sworn deceitfully.

—PSALM 24:3–4

The wisdom of the prudent is to understand his way, but the folly of fools is deceit. Fools make a mock at sin, but among the righteous there is favor.

—PROVERBS 14:8–9

Therefore, everything you would like men to do to you, do also to them, for this is the Law and the Prophets.

—MATTHEW 7:12

Jesus said to him, "'You shall love the Lord your God with all your heart, and with all your soul, and with all your mind.' This is the first and great commandment. And the second is like it: 'You shall love your neighbor as yourself.' On these two commandments hang all the Law and the Prophets."

—MATTHEW 22:37–40

CHARITY

Blessed are those who consider the poor; the Lord will deliver them in the day of trouble. The Lord will preserve them and keep them alive, and they will be blessed on the earth, and You will not deliver them to the will of their enemies.

—Psalm 41:1–2

There is one who scatters, yet increases; and there is one who withholds more than is right, but it leads to poverty. The generous soul will be made rich, and he who waters will be watered also himself.

—Proverbs 11:24–25

He who has pity on the poor lends to the Lord, and He will repay what he has given.

—Proverbs 19:17

Be sure that you not do your charitable deeds before men to be seen by them. Otherwise you have no reward from your Father who is in heaven. Therefore, when you do your charitable deeds, do not sound a trumpet before you as the hypocrites do in the synagogues and in the streets, that they may be honored by men. Truly I say to you, they have their reward. But when you do your charitable deeds, do not let your left hand know what your right hand is doing, that your charitable deeds may be in secret. And your Father who sees in secret will Himself reward you openly.

—Matthew 6:1–4

Give, and it will be given to you: Good measure, pressed down, shaken together, and running over, will men give unto you. For with the measure you use, it will be measured unto you.

—Luke 6:38

CHEATING

Lying lips are abomination to the Lord, but those who deal truly are His delight.

—Proverbs 12:22

Better is the poor who walks in his integrity, than he who is perverse in his lips and is a fool.

—Proverbs 19:1

He who is faithful in what is least is faithful also in much. And he who is dishonest in the least is dishonest also in much. So if you have not been faithful in the unrighteous wealth, who will commit to your trust the true riches? And if you have not been faithful in that which is another man's, who will give you that which is your own?

—Luke 16:10–12

Be not deceived. God is not mocked. For whatever a man sows, that will he also reap. For the one who sows to his own flesh will from the flesh reap corruption, but the one who sows to the Spirit will from the Spirit reap eternal life.

—Galatians 6:7–8

Therefore, to him who knows to do good and does not do it, it is sin.

—James 4:17

CHRISTIAN FELLOWSHIP

Be devoted to one another with brotherly love; prefer one another in honor.

—Romans 12:10

Truly the signs of an apostle were performed among you in all patience, in signs and wonders, and mighty deeds.

—2 Corinthians 12:12

Now we command you, brothers, in the name of our Lord Jesus Christ, that you withdraw yourselves from every brother who walks in idleness and not according to the tradition that he received from us.

—2 Thessalonians 3:6

And let us consider how to spur one another to love and to good works. Let us not forsake the assembling of ourselves together, as is the manner of some, but let us exhort one another, especially as you see the Day approaching.

—Hebrews 10:24–25

We declare to you that which we have seen and heard, that you also may have fellowship with us. And our fellowship is with the Father and with His Son Jesus Christ.

—1 John 1:3

COMMITMENT

See, I am setting before you today a blessing and a curse: the blessing if you obey the commandments of the LORD your God, which I am commanding you today, and the curse, if you will not obey the commandments of the LORD your God, but turn from the way which I am commanding you today, to go after other gods which you have not known.

—DEUTERONOMY 11:26–28

Samuel said, "Does the LORD delight in burnt offerings and sacrifices as much as in obeying the voice of the LORD? Obedience is better than sacrifice, a listening ear than the fat of rams."

—1 SAMUEL 15:22

And I will give them one heart and one way, that they may fear Me forever, for their good and for their children after them. And I will make an everlasting covenant with them that I will not turn away from them, to do them good. But I will put My fear in their hearts so that they shall not depart from Me.

—JEREMIAH 32:39–40

But let your "Yes" mean "Yes," and "No" mean "No." For whatever is more than these comes from the evil one.

—MATTHEW 5:37

Whoever will confess Me before men, him will I confess also before My Father who is in heaven. But whoever will deny

Me before men, him will I also deny before My Father who is in heaven.

—Matthew 10:32–33

COMPASSION

Nothing of the cursed thing there must cling to your hand, so that the Lord may turn from the fierceness of His anger and show you mercy, have compassion on you, and multiply you, just as He swore to your fathers.

—Deuteronomy 13:17

A good man shows generous favor, and lends; he will guide his affairs with justice.

—Psalm 112:5

He who has pity on the poor lends to the Lord, and He will repay what he has given.

—Proverbs 19:17

Thus says the Lord of Hosts: Execute true justice, show mercy and compassion, every man to his brother. Do not oppress the widow, orphan, sojourner, or poor. And let none of you contemplate evil deeds in your hearts against his brother.

—Zechariah 7:9–10

So embrace, as the elect of God, holy and beloved, a spirit of mercy, kindness, humbleness of mind, meekness, and longsuffering.

—Colossians 3:12

Religion that is pure and undefiled before God, the Father, is this: to visit the fatherless and widows in their affliction and to keep oneself unstained by the world.

—James 1:27

COMPETITION

Do you not know that all those who run in a race run, but one receives the prize? So run, that you may obtain it.

—1 Corinthians 9:24

Let nothing be done out of strife or conceit, but in humility let each esteem the other better than himself. Let each of you look not only to your own interests, but also to the interests of others.

—Philippians 2:3–4

I can do all things because of Christ who strengthens me.

—Philippians 4:13

And whatever you do, do it heartily, as for the Lord and not for men.

—Colossians 3:23

Anyone who competes as an athlete is not rewarded without competing legally.

—2 Timothy 2:5

But He gives more grace. For this reason it says: "God resists the proud, but gives grace to the humble."

—James 4:6

COMPLAINING

Let no unwholesome word proceed out of your mouth, but only that which is good for building up, that it may give grace to the listeners.

—Ephesians 4:29

Do all things without murmuring and disputing.

—Philippians 2:14

In everything give thanks, for this is the will of God in Christ Jesus concerning you.

—1 Thessalonians 5:18

Do not grumble against one another, brothers, lest you be condemned. Look, the Judge is standing at the door.

—James 5:9

Show hospitality to one another without complaining. As everyone has received a gift, even so serve one another with it, as good stewards of the manifold grace of God.

—1 Peter 4:9–10

COMPROMISE

Now fear the LORD, and serve Him with sincerity and faithfulness. Put away the gods your fathers served beyond the River and in Egypt. Serve the LORD. If it is displeasing to you to serve the LORD, then choose today whom you will serve, if it should be the gods your fathers served beyond the River or the gods of the Amorites' land where you are now living. Yet as for me and my house, we will serve the LORD.

—JOSHUA 24:14–15

If you love Me, keep My commandments.

—JOHN 14:15

Welcome him who is weak in faith, but not for the purpose of arguing over opinions. For one has faith to eat all things, but he who is weak eats only vegetables. Do not let him who eats despise him who does not eat, and do not let him who does not eat judge him who eats, for God has welcomed him. Who are you to judge another man's servant? To his own master he stands or falls. And he will stand, for God is able to make him stand.

—ROMANS 14:1–4

For if we willfully continue to sin after we have received the knowledge of the truth, there no longer remains a sacrifice for sins.

—HEBREWS 10:26

Therefore, to him who knows to do good and does not do it, it is sin.

—James 4:17

CONDEMNATION

Who is he who condemns? It is Christ who died, yes, who is risen, who is also at the right hand of God, who also intercedes for us.

—Romans 8:34

If I speak with the tongues of men and of angels, and have not love, I have become as sounding brass or a clanging cymbal.

—1 Corinthians 13:1

Now this is the main point of the things that we are saying: We have such a High Priest, who is seated at the right hand of the throne of the Majesty in the heavens, a minister in the sanctuary and the true tabernacle, which the Lord, not man, set up.

—Hebrews 8:1–2

If we confess our sins, He is faithful and just to forgive us our sins and cleanse us from all unrighteousness.

—1 John 1:9

There shall be no more curse. The throne of God and of the Lamb shall be in it, and His servants shall serve Him. They shall see His face, and His name shall be on their foreheads.

—Revelation 22:3–4

CONFIDENCE

For You are my hope, O Lord God; You are my confidence from my youth.

—Psalm 71:5

It is better to trust in the Lord than to put confidence in man. It is better to trust in the Lord than to put confidence in princes.

—Psalm 118:8–9

In the fear of the Lord is strong confidence, and His children will have a place of refuge.

—Proverbs 14:26

Therefore do not throw away your confidence, which will be greatly rewarded.

—Hebrews 10:35

And now, little children, remain in Him, so that when He appears, we may have confidence and not be ashamed before Him when He comes.

—1 John 2:28

Beloved, if our heart does not condemn us, then we have confidence before God.

—1 John 3:21

This is the confidence that we have in Him, that if we ask anything according to His will, He hears us. So if we know that

He hears whatever we ask, we know that we have whatever we asked of Him.

—1 John 5:14–15

CONFLICT

Be angry but do not sin. Do not let the sun go down on your anger. Do not give place to the devil.

—Ephesians 4:26–27

Let all bitterness, wrath, anger, outbursts, and blasphemies, with all malice, be taken away from you. And be kind one to another, tenderhearted, forgiving one another, just as God in Christ also forgave you.

—Ephesians 4:31–32

Let everyone come to know your gentleness. The Lord is at hand.

—Philippians 4:5

Therefore, my beloved brothers, let every man be swift to hear, slow to speak, and slow to anger, for the anger of man does not work the righteousness of God.

—James 1:19–20

Finally, be all of one mind, be loving toward one another, be gracious, and be kind. Do not repay evil for evil, or curse for curse, but on the contrary, bless, knowing that to this you are called, so that you may receive a blessing.

—1 Peter 3:8–9

CONFUSION

But when the Spirit of truth comes, He will guide you into all truth. For He will not speak on His own authority. But He will speak whatever He hears, and He will tell you things that are to come.

—John 16:13

I urge you therefore, brothers, by the mercies of God, that you present your bodies as a living sacrifice, holy, and acceptable to God, which is your reasonable service of worship. Do not be conformed to this world, but be transformed by the renewing of your mind, that you may prove what is the good and acceptable and perfect will of God.

—Romans 12:1–2

For God is not the author of confusion, but of peace, as in all churches of the saints.

—1 Corinthians 14:33

Finally, brothers, whatever things are true, whatever things are honest, whatever things are just, whatever things are pure, whatever things are lovely, whatever things are of good report, if there is any virtue, and if there is any praise, think on these things. Do those things which you have both learned and received, and heard and seen in me, and the God of peace will be with you.

—Philippians 4:8–9

Be sober and watchful, because your adversary the devil walks around as a roaring lion, seeking whom he may devour.

—1 Peter 5:8

Beloved, do not believe every spirit, but test the spirits to see whether they are from God, because many false prophets have gone out into the world.

—1 John 4:1

CONTENTMENT

The Lord is the portion of my inheritance and of my cup; You support my lot. The lines have fallen for me in pleasant places; yes, an inheritance is beautiful for me.

—Psalm 16:5–6

Rest in the Lord, and wait patiently for Him; do not fret because of those who prosper in their way, because of those who make wicked schemes. Let go of anger, and forsake wrath; do not fret—it surely leads to evil deeds. For evildoers will be cut off, but those who hope in the Lord will inherit the earth.

—Psalm 37:7–9

The backslider in heart will be filled with his own ways, but a good man will be satisfied with his.

—Proverbs 14:14

I do not speak because I have need, for I have learned in whatever state I am to be content. I know both how to face humble circumstances and how to have abundance. Everywhere and in all things I have learned the secret, both to be full and to be hungry, both to abound and to suffer need. I can do all things because of Christ who strengthens me.

—Philippians 4:11–13

Let your lives be without love of money, and be content with the things you have. For He has said: "I will never leave you, nor forsake you."

—Hebrews 13:5

COURAGE

But now, thus says the Lord who created you, O Jacob, and He who formed you, O Israel: Do not fear, for I have redeemed you; I have called you by your name; you are Mine.

—Isaiah 43:1

In all these things we are more than conquerors through Him who loved us. For I am persuaded that neither death nor life, neither angels nor principalities nor powers, neither things present nor things to come, neither height nor depth, nor any other created thing, shall be able to separate us from the love of God, which is in Christ Jesus our Lord.

—Romans 8:37–39

Watch, stand fast in the faith, be bold like men, and be strong.

—1 Corinthians 16:13

Finally, my brothers, be strong in the Lord and in the power of His might.

—Ephesians 6:10

Beloved, do not be surprised at the fiery ordeal that is taking place among you to test you, as though some strange thing happened to you. But rejoice insofar as you share in Christ's sufferings, so that you may rejoice and be glad also in the revelation of His glory.

—1 Peter 4:12–13

CREATIVITY

And He has filled him with the Spirit of God, in wisdom, in understanding, and in knowledge, and in all manner of craftsmanship, to design artistic works, to work in gold, in silver, and in bronze, and in the cutting of stones for settings and in the carving of wood in order to make every manner of artistic work.

—Exodus 35:31–33

There are various gifts, but the same Spirit. There are differences of administrations, but the same Lord. There are various operations, but it is the same God who operates all of them in all people.

—1 Corinthians 12:4–6

For if there is a willing mind first, the gift is accepted according to what a man possesses and not according to what he does not possess.

—2 Corinthians 8:12

Every good gift and every perfect gift is from above and comes down from the Father of lights, with whom is no change or shadow of turning.

—James 1:17

As everyone has received a gift, even so serve one another with it, as good stewards of the manifold grace of God. If anyone speaks, let him speak as the oracles of God. If anyone serves, let him serve with the strength that God supplies, so that God in all things may be glorified through Jesus Christ, to whom be praise and dominion forever and ever.

—1 Peter 4:10–11

CRISIS

The righteous cry out, and the Lord hears, and delivers them out of all their troubles. The Lord is near to the broken-hearted, and saves the contrite of spirit. Many are the afflictions of the righteous, but the Lord delivers him out of them all. A righteous one keeps all his bones; not one of them is broken.

—Psalm 34:17–20

But he who endures to the end shall be saved.

—Matthew 24:13

Therefore watch always and pray that you may be counted worthy to escape all these things that will happen and to stand before the Son of Man.

—Luke 21:36

He said to them, "It is not for you to know the times or the dates, which the Father has fixed by His own authority. But you shall receive power when the Holy Spirit comes upon you. And you shall be My witnesses in Jerusalem, and in all Judea and Samaria, and to the ends of the earth."

—Acts 1:7–8

But my God shall supply your every need according to His riches in glory by Christ Jesus.

—Philippians 4:19

CRITICISM

O Lord my God, in You I put my trust; save me from all those who persecute me, and deliver me.

—Psalm 7:1

When pride comes, then comes shame; but with the humble is wisdom.

—Proverbs 11:2

Blessed are you when men revile you, and persecute you, and say all kinds of evil against you falsely for My sake.

—Matthew 5:11

You have heard that it was said, "You shall love your neighbor and hate your enemy." But I say to you, love your enemies, bless those who curse you, do good to those who hate you, and pray for those who spitefully use you and persecute you.

—Matthew 5:43–44

Remember the word that I said to you: "A servant is not greater than his master." If they persecuted Me, they will also persecute you. If they kept My words, they will keep yours also.

—John 15:20

DECEIT

You shall not steal, nor deal falsely, nor lie to one another.

—Leviticus 19:11

He who practices deceit shall not dwell within my house; he who tells lies shall not remain in my sight.

—Psalm 101:7

Charm is deceitful, and beauty is vain, but a woman who fears the Lord, she shall be praised.

—Proverbs 31:30

The heart is more deceitful than all things and desperately wicked; who can understand it? I, the Lord, search the heart, I test the mind, even to give to every man according to his ways, and according to the fruit of his deeds.

—Jeremiah 17:9–10

Let no one deceive you with empty words, for because of these things the wrath of God is coming upon the sons of disobedience.

—Ephesians 5:6

DEFEAT

He also brought me up out of a horrible pit, out of the miry clay, and set my feet on a rock, and established my steps. He has put a new song in my mouth, even praise to our God; many will see it, and fear, and will trust in the Lord.

—Psalm 40:2–3

For a just man falls seven times and rises up again, but the wicked will fall into mischief.

—Proverbs 24:16

Beloved, do not avenge yourselves, but rather give place to God's wrath, for it is written: "Vengeance is Mine. I will repay," says the Lord.

—Romans 12:19

Now therefore it is already an utter failure for you that you go to law against one another. Why not rather be wronged? Why not rather be defrauded? But you yourselves do wrong and defraud, and do this to your brothers.

—1 Corinthians 6:7–8

But He said to me, "My grace is sufficient for you, for My strength is made perfect in weakness." Therefore most gladly

I will boast in my weaknesses, that the power of Christ may rest upon me.

—2 Corinthians 12:9

DELIVERANCE

He said: The Lord is my rock and my fortress and my deliverer.
—2 Samuel 22:2

With the merciful You will show Yourself merciful; with the blameless man You will show Yourself blameless.

—Psalm 18:25

For You will cause my lamp to shine; the Lord my God will enlighten my darkness. For by You I can run through a troop, and by my God I can leap a wall.

—Psalm 18:28–29

I will bless the Lord at all times; His praise will continually be in my mouth. My soul will make its boast in the Lord; the humble will hear of it and be glad. Oh, magnify the Lord with me, and let us exalt His name together. I sought the Lord, and He answered me, and delivered me from all my fears. They looked to Him and became radiant, and their faces are not ashamed. This poor man cried, and the Lord heard, and saved him out of all his troubles.

—Psalm 34:1–6

Many are the afflictions of the righteous, but the Lord delivers him out of them all. A righteous one keeps all his bones; not one of them is broken. Evil will slay the wicked, and those who hate the righteous will be condemned. The Lord redeems the life of His servants, and all who take refuge in Him will not be punished.

—Psalm 34:19–22

DENIAL

I am the Lord your God, who brought you out of the land of Egypt, out of the house of bondage. You shall have no other gods before Me. You shall not make for yourself any graven idol, or any likeness of anything that is in heaven above, or that is in the earth beneath, or that is in the water below the earth. You shall not bow down to them or serve them; for I, the Lord your God, am a jealous God, visiting the iniquity of the fathers on the children to the third and fourth generation of them who hate Me, and showing lovingkindness to thousands of them who love Me and keep My commandments.

—Exodus 20:2–6

Now it will be, if you will diligently obey the voice of the Lord your God, being careful to do all His commandments which I am commanding you today, then the Lord your God will set you high above all the nations of the earth.

—Deuteronomy 28:1

For I am persuaded that neither death nor life, neither angels nor principalities nor powers, neither things present nor things to come, neither height nor depth, nor any other created thing, shall be able to separate us from the love of God, which is in Christ Jesus our Lord.

—Romans 8:38–39

But whoever will deny Me before men, him will I also deny before My Father who is in heaven.

—Matthew 10:33

Then He said to them all, "If anyone will come after Me, let him deny himself, and take up his cross daily, and follow Me."

—Luke 9:23

DEPRESSION

When I said, "My foot slips," Your mercy, O Lord, held me up. When there is a multitude of worries within me, Your comforts delight my soul.

—Psalm 94:18–19

For I will set My eyes upon them for good, and I will bring them again to this land. And I will build them up and not pull them down. And I will plant them and not pluck them up. I will give them a heart to know Me, that I am the Lord; and they will be My people, and I will be their God, for they will return to Me with their whole heart.

—Jeremiah 24:6–7

Come to Me, all you who labor and are heavily burdened, and I will give you rest. Take My yoke upon you, and learn from

Me. For I am meek and lowly in heart, and you will find rest for your souls.

—Matthew 11:28–29

Nevertheless when anyone turns to the Lord, the veil is removed. Now the Lord is the Spirit. And where the Spirit of the Lord is, there is liberty.

—2 Corinthians 3:16–17

Be anxious for nothing, but in everything, by prayer and supplication with gratitude, make your requests known to God. And the peace of God, which surpasses all understanding, will protect your hearts and minds through Christ Jesus.

—Philippians 4:6–7

DIFFERENCES

You shall not take vengeance, nor bear any grudge against the children of your people, but you shall love your neighbor as yourself: I am the Lord.

—Leviticus 19:18

For if you forgive men for their sins, your heavenly Father will also forgive you. But if you do not forgive men for their sins, neither will your Father forgive your sins.

—Matthew 6:14–15

He looked up and saw the rich putting their gifts in the treasury. He also saw a poor widow putting in two mites, and He said, "Truly I tell you, this poor widow has put in more than all of them. For all these out of their abundance have put in their gifts for God. But she out of her poverty has put in all the living she had."

—Luke 21:1–4

I can do nothing of Myself. As I hear, I judge. My judgment is just, because I seek not My own will, but the will of the Father who sent Me.

—John 5:30

Do not be unequally yoked together with unbelievers. For what fellowship has righteousness with unrighteousness? What communion has light with darkness?

—2 Corinthians 6:14

There is neither Jew nor Greek, there is neither slave nor free, and there is neither male nor female, for you are all one in Christ Jesus.

—Galatians 3:28

DISCIPLESHIP

Whoever hears these sayings of Mine and does them, I will liken him to a wise man who built his house on a rock. And the rain descended, the floods came, and the winds blew and beat on that house. And it did not fall, for it was founded a rock.

—Matthew 7:24–25

For those who live according to the flesh set their minds on the things of the flesh, but those who live according to the Spirit, the things of the Spirit.

—Romans 8:5

For the one who sows to his own flesh will from the flesh reap corruption, but the one who sows to the Spirit will from the Spirit reap eternal life. And let us not grow weary in doing good, for in due season we shall reap, if we do not give up.

—Galatians 6:8–9

Brothers, I do not count myself to have attained, but this one thing I do, forgetting those things which are behind and reaching forward to those things which are ahead, I press toward the goal to the prize of the high calling of God in Christ Jesus.

—Philippians 3:13–14

For the grace of God that brings salvation has appeared to all men, teaching us that, denying ungodliness and worldly desires, we should live soberly, righteously, and in godliness in this present world.

—Titus 2:11–12

DISCOURAGEMENT

I cried out to God with my voice, even to God with my voice; and He listened to me.

—Psalm 77:1

He heals the broken in heart, and binds up their wounds.

—Psalm 147:3

A merry heart does good like a medicine, but a broken spirit dries the bones.

—Proverbs 17:22

But those who wait upon the Lord shall renew their strength; they shall mount up with wings as eagles, they shall run and not be weary, and they shall walk and not faint.

—Isaiah 40:31

We are troubled on every side, yet not distressed; we are perplexed, but not in despair; persecuted, but not forsaken; cast down, but not destroyed; and always carrying around in the body the death of the Lord Jesus, that also the life of Jesus might be expressed in our bodies.

—2 Corinthians 4:8–10

Knowing that He who raised the Lord Jesus will also raise us through Jesus and will present us with you.

—2 Corinthians 4:14

DISTRESS

When the poor and needy seek water, and there is none, and their tongues fail for thirst, I, the Lord, will hear them, I, the God of Israel, will not forsake them.

—Isaiah 41:17

He lifted up His eyes on His disciples, and said: "Blessed are you poor, for yours is the kingdom of God. Blessed are you who hunger now, for you shall be filled. Blessed are you who weep now, for you shall laugh."

—Luke 6:20–21

Do not work for the food which perishes, but for that food which endures to eternal life, which the Son of Man will give you. For God the Father has set His seal on Him.

—John 6:27

Listen, my beloved brothers. Has God not chosen the poor of this world to be rich in faith and heirs of the kingdom which He has promised to those who love Him?

—James 2:5

But rejoice insofar as you share in Christ's sufferings, so that you may rejoice and be glad also in the revelation of His glory.

—1 Peter 4:13

DIVORCE

Therefore a man will leave his father and his mother and be joined to his wife, and they will become one flesh.

—Genesis 2:24

It was said, "Whoever divorces his wife, let him give her a certificate of divorce." But I say to you that whoever divorces his wife, except for marital unfaithfulness, causes her to commit adultery. And whoever marries her who is divorced commits adultery.

—Matthew 5:31–32

He said to them, "Moses, for the hardness of your hearts, permitted you to divorce your wives, but from the beginning it was not so. But I say to you, whoever divorces his wife, except for sexual immorality, and marries another, commits adultery. And whoever marries her who is divorced commits adultery."

—Matthew 19:8–9

Now to the married I command, not I, but the Lord, do not let the wife depart from her husband. But if she departs, let her remain unmarried or be reconciled to her husband. And do not let the husband divorce his wife.

—1 Corinthians 7:10–11

But if the unbeliever departs, let that one depart. A brother or a sister is not bound in such cases. God has called us to peace. 16 For how do you know, O wife, whether you will save your husband? Or how do you know, O husband, whether you will save your wife?

—1 Corinthians 7:15–16

Marriage is to be honored among everyone, and the bed undefiled. But God will judge the sexually immoral and adulterers.

—Hebrews 13:4

DOUBT

He replied, "Why are you fearful, O you of little faith?" Then He rose and rebuked the winds and the sea. And there was a great calm.

—Matthew 8:26

Jesus said to him, "Thomas, because you have seen Me, you have believed. Blessed are those who have not seen, and have yet believed."

—John 20:29

And without faith it is impossible to please God, for he who comes to God must believe that He exists and that He is a rewarder of those who diligently seek Him.

—Hebrews 11:6

Therefore, since we are encompassed with such a great cloud of witnesses, let us also lay aside every weight and the sin that so easily entangles us, and let us run with endurance the race that is set before us. Let us look to Jesus, the author and finisher of our faith, who for the joy that was set before Him endured the cross, despising the shame, and is seated at the right hand of the throne of God.

—Hebrews 12:1–2

A double-minded man is unstable in all his ways.

—James 1:8

DREAMS AND VISIONS

Where there is no vision, the people perish; but happy is he who keeps the teaching.

—Proverbs 29:18

As for these four youths, God gave them knowledge and skill in every branch of learning and wisdom. And Daniel had understanding in all kinds of visions and dreams.

—Daniel 1:17

And it will be that, afterwards, I will pour out My Spirit on all flesh; then your sons and your daughters will prophesy, your old men will dream dreams, and your young men will see visions.

—Joel 2:28

Surely the Lord God does nothing without revealing His purpose to His servants the prophets.

—Amos 3:7

"In the last days it shall be," says God, "that I will pour out My Spirit on all flesh; your sons and your daughters shall prophesy, your young men shall see visions, and your old men shall dream dreams. Even on My menservants and maidservants I will pour out My Spirit in those days; and they shall prophesy."

—Acts 2:17–18

EGO

Do you see a man wise in his own conceit? There is more hope for a fool than for him.

—Proverbs 26:12

The sluggard is wiser in his own conceit than seven men who can answer reasonably.

—Proverbs 26:16

Even the youths shall faint and be weary, and the young men shall utterly fall, but those who wait upon the Lord shall renew their strength; they shall mount up with wings as eagles, they shall run and not be weary, and they shall walk and not faint.

—Isaiah 40:30–31

I can do nothing of Myself. As I hear, I judge. My judgment is just, because I seek not My own will, but the will of the Father who sent Me.

—John 5:30

Let nothing be done out of strife or conceit, but in humility let each esteem the other better than himself. Let each of you look not only to your own interests, but also to the interests of others. Let this mind be in you all, which was also in Christ Jesus.

—Philippians 2:3–5

EMPLOYER/EMPLOYEES

You shall not rule over him with harshness, but you shall fear your God.

—Leviticus 25:43

You may not oppress a hired servant that is poor and needy, whether he is one of your brothers or one of your foreigners who are in your land within your towns. You must give him his wages on that very day before the sun sets, for he is poor, and sets his heart on it, lest he cry against you to the Lord, and it be a sin to you.

—Deuteronomy 24:14–15

Therefore, everything you would like men to do to you, do also to them, for this is the Law and the Prophets.

—Matthew 7:12

Servants, obey your masters in all things according to the flesh, serving not only when they are watching, as the servants of men, but in singleness of heart, fearing God. And whatever you do, do it heartily, as for the Lord and not for men.

—Colossians 3:22–23

For the Scripture says, "You shall not muzzle the ox that treads out the grain," and, "The laborer is worthy of his reward."

—1 Timothy 5:18

ENCOURAGEMENT

Heaviness in the heart of man makes it droop, but a good word makes it glad.

—Proverbs 12:25

But this I call to mind, and therefore I have hope: It is of the Lord's mercies that we are not consumed; His compassions do not fail. They are new every morning; great is Your faithfulness.

—Lamentations 3:21–23

God is faithful, and by Him you were called to the fellowship of His Son, Jesus Christ our Lord.

—1 Corinthians 1:9

Now may our Lord Jesus Christ Himself, and God our Father, who has loved us and has given us eternal consolation and good hope through grace, comfort your hearts and establish you in every good word and work.

—2 Thessalonians 2:16–17

And let us consider how to spur one another to love and to good works.

—Hebrews 10:24

ENDURANCE

Not only so, but we also boast in tribulation, knowing that tribulation produces patience, patience produces character, and character produces hope.

—Romans 5:3–4

No temptation has taken you except what is common to man. God is faithful, and He will not permit you to be tempted above what you can endure, but will with the temptation also make a way to escape, that you may be able to bear it.

—1 Corinthians 10:13

Strengthened with all might according to His glorious power, enduring everything with perseverance and patience joyfully.

—Colossians 1:11

For you need patience, so that after you have done the will of God, you will receive the promise.

—Hebrews 10:36

Blessed is the man who endures temptation, for when he is tried, he will receive the crown of life, which the Lord has promised to those who love Him.

—James 1:12

ENVY

A sound heart is the life of the flesh, but envy the rottenness of the bones.

—PROVERBS 14:30

Do not let your heart envy sinners, but continue in the fear of the LORD all day long.

—PROVERBS 23:17

Wrath is cruel, and anger is outrageous, but who is able to stand before envy?

—PROVERBS 27:4

And do not let sexual immorality, or any impurity, or greed be named among you, as these are not proper among saints.

—EPHESIANS 5:3

Let your lives be without love of money, and be content with the things you have. For He has said: "I will never leave you, nor forsake you."

—HEBREWS 13:5

For where there is envying and strife, there is confusion and every evil work.

—JAMES 3:16

ETERNAL LIFE

Many of those who sleep in the dust of the earth shall awake, some to everlasting life, but others to shame and everlasting contempt.

—Daniel 12:2

Therefore, brothers, let it be known to you that through this Man forgiveness of sins is proclaimed to you, and by Him everyone who believes is justified from everything from which you could not be justified by the Law of Moses.

—Acts 13:38–39

So also is the resurrection of the dead. The body is sown in corruption; it is raised in incorruption. It is sown in dishonor, it is raised in glory. It is sown in weakness, it is raised in power. It is sown a natural body, it is raised a spiritual body. There is a natural body, and there is a spiritual body.

—1 Corinthians 15:42–44

But is now revealed by the appearing of our Savior, Jesus Christ, who has abolished death and has brought life and immortality to light through the gospel.

—2 Timothy 1:10

I have written these things to you who believe in the name of the Son of God, that you may know that you have eternal life, and that you may continue to believe in the name of the Son of God.

—1 John 5:13

EXCUSES

Not everyone who says to Me, "Lord, Lord," shall enter the kingdom of heaven, but he who does the will of My Father who is in heaven.

—Matthew 7:21

He said to another man, "Follow Me." But he said, "Lord, let me first go and bury my father." Jesus said to him, "Leave the dead to bury their own dead. But you go and preach the kingdom of God." Yet another said, "Lord, I will follow You, but let me first go bid farewell to those at my house." Jesus said to him, "No one who puts his hand to the plow and looks back at things is fit for the kingdom of God."

—Luke 9:59–62

Therefore you are without excuse, O man, whoever you are who judges, for when you judge another, you condemn yourself, for you who judge do the same things.

—Romans 2:1

Follow me as I follow Christ. I praise you, brothers, that you remember me in all things and keep the traditions as I delivered them to you.

—1 Corinthians 11:1–2

Therefore, if any man is in Christ, he is a new creature. Old things have passed away. Look, all things have become new.

—2 Corinthians 5:17

EXPECTATIONS

For surely there is an end, and your expectation will not be cut off.

—Proverbs 23:18

For I know the plans that I have for you, says the Lord, plans for peace and not for evil, to give you a future and a hope.

—Jeremiah 29:11

Come to Me, all you who labor and are heavily burdened, and I will give you rest.

—Matthew 11:28

Accordingly, it is my earnest expectation and my hope that I shall be ashamed in nothing, but that with all boldness as always, so now also, Christ will be magnified in my body, whether it be by life or by death.

—Philippians 1:20

Be anxious for nothing, but in everything, by prayer and supplication with gratitude, make your requests known to God.

—Philippians 4:6

FAILURE

Then David said to Solomon his son, "Be strong and courageous, and take action. Do not be afraid nor be dismayed for the Lord God, my God, is with you. He will not leave you nor forsake you, until you have finished all the work of the service of the house of the LORD."

—1 CHRONICLES 28:20

All these things are for your sakes, so that the abundant grace through the thanksgiving of many might overflow to the glory of God. For this reason we do not lose heart: Even though our outward man is perishing, yet our inward man is being renewed day by day.

—2 CORINTHIANS 4:15–16

But He said to me, "My grace is sufficient for you, for My strength is made perfect in weakness." Therefore most gladly I will boast in my weaknesses, that the power of Christ may rest upon me.

—2 CORINTHIANS 12:9

I can do all things because of Christ who strengthens me.

—PHILIPPIANS 4:13

For we do not have a High Priest who cannot sympathize with our weaknesses, but One who was in every sense tempted like we are, yet without sin. Let us then come with confidence to the throne of grace, that we may obtain mercy and find grace to help in time of need.

—HEBREWS 4:15–16

FAIRNESS

Blessed are those who keep justice and who do righteousness at all times.

—Psalm 106:3

A just weight and balance belong to the Lord; all the weights of the bag are His work.

—Proverbs 16:11

Again I saw under the sun that—the race is not to the swift, nor the battle to the strong, nor food to the wise, nor riches to the intelligent, nor favor to those with knowledge; but time and chance happen to them all.

—Ecclesiastes 9:11

For God is not unjust so as to forget your work and labor of love that you have shown for His name, in that you have ministered to the saints and continue ministering.

—Hebrews 6:10

For if a man with a gold ring, in fine clothing, comes into your assembly, and also a poor man in ragged clothing comes in, and you have respect for him who wears the fine clothing and say to him, "Sit here in a good place," and say to the poor, "Stand there," or "Sit here under my footstool," have you not then become partial among yourselves and become judges with evil thoughts?

—James 2:2–4

FAITH

Jesus said to them, "Because of your unbelief. For truly I say to you, if you have faith as a grain of mustard seed, you will say to this mountain, 'Move from here to there,' and it will move. And nothing will be impossible for you."

—Matthew 17:20

But to him who does not work, but believes in Him who justifies the ungodly, his faith is credited as righteousness.

—Romans 4:5

For by grace you have been saved through faith, and this is not of yourselves. It is the gift of God.

—Ephesians 2:8

But continue in the things that you have learned and have been assured of, knowing those from whom you have learned them, and that since childhood you have known the Holy Scriptures, which are able to make you wise unto salvation through the faith that is in Christ Jesus.

—2 Timothy 3:14–15

If any of you lacks wisdom, let him ask of God, who gives to all men liberally and without criticism, and it will be given to him. But let him ask in faith, without wavering. For he who wavers is like a wave of the sea, driven and tossed with the wind.

—James 1:5–6

FATHERHOOD

Hear me when I call, O God of my righteousness! You have given me relief when I was in distress; have mercy on me, and hear my prayer. O people, how long will you turn my glory into shame? How long will you love vanity and seek after lies? Selah

—Psalm 4:1–2

Like a father shows compassion to his children, so the Lord gives compassion to those who fear Him.

—Psalm 103:13

He who spares his rod hates his son, but he who loves him disciplines him early.

—Proverbs 13:24

The just man walks in his integrity; his children are blessed after him.

—Proverbs 20:7

Have we not all one Father? Has not one God created us? Why do we deal treacherously with one another, by profaning the covenant of our fathers?

—Malachi 2:10

Fathers, do not provoke your children to anger, but bring them up in the discipline and instruction of the Lord.

—Ephesians 6:4

FEAR

The Lord is my light and my salvation; whom will I fear? The Lord is the strength of my life; of whom will I be afraid? When the wicked came against me to eat my flesh—my enemies and my foes—they stumbled and fell. Though an army should encamp against me, my heart will not fear; though war should rise against me, in this will I be confident.

—Psalm 27:1–3

The fear of man brings a snare, but whoever puts his trust in the Lord will be safe.

—Proverbs 29:25

When you pass through waters, I will be with you. And through the rivers, they shall not overflow you. When you walk through the fire, you shall not be burned, nor shall the flame kindle on you.

—Isaiah 43:2

Do not fear those who kill the body but are not able to kill the soul. But rather fear Him who is able to destroy both soul and body in hell.

—Matthew 10:28

No, in all these things we are more than conquerors through Him who loved us. For I am persuaded that neither death nor life, neither angels nor principalities nor powers, neither things present nor things to come, neither height nor depth,

nor any other created thing, shall be able to separate us from
the love of God, which is in Christ Jesus our Lord.

—Romans 8:37–39

FINANCIAL TROUBLE

Wealth gained by vanity will be diminished, but he who
gathers by labor will increase.

—Proverbs 13:11

Bring all the tithes into the storehouse, that there may be food
in My house, and test Me now in this, says the Lord of Hosts,
if I will not open for you the windows of heaven and pour
out for you a blessing, that there will not be room enough to
receive it. I will rebuke the devourer for your sakes, so that it
will not destroy the fruit of your ground, and the vines in your
field will not fail to bear fruit, says the Lord of Hosts.

—Malachi 3:10–11

I do not speak because I have need, for I have learned in whatever state I am to be content. I know both how to face humble
circumstances and how to have abundance. Everywhere and in
all things I have learned the secret, both to be full and to be
hungry, both to abound and to suffer need. I can do all things
because of Christ who strengthens me.

—Philippians 4:11–13

But my God shall supply your every need according to His riches in glory by Christ Jesus.

—Philippians 4:19

Let your lives be without love of money, and be content with the things you have. For He has said: "I will never leave you, nor forsake you." So we may boldly say: "The Lord is my helper; I will not fear. What can man do to me?"

—Hebrews 13:5–6

FINDING GOD IN THE VALLEYS

Even though I walk through the valley of the shadow of death, I will fear no evil for You are with me; Your rod and Your staff, they comfort me.

—Psalm 23:4

Do not neglect the gift that is in you, which was given to you by prophecy, with the laying on of hands by the elders.

—1 Timothy 414

Every good gift and every perfect gift is from above and comes down from the Father of lights, with whom is no change or shadow of turning.

—James 1:17

As everyone has received a gift, even so serve one another with it, as good stewards of the manifold grace of God.

—1 Peter 4:10

FORGIVENESS

Take heed to yourselves. "If your brother sins against you, rebuke him. And if he repents, forgive him. If he sins against you seven times in a day, and seven times in a day turns to you, saying, 'I repent,' you must forgive him."

—Luke 17:3–4

And be kind one to another, tenderhearted, forgiving one another, just as God in Christ also forgave you.

—Ephesians 4:32

Bear with one another and forgive one another. If anyone has a quarrel against anyone, even as Christ forgave you, so you must do.

—Colossians 3:13

For I will be merciful toward their unrighteousness, and their sins and their lawless deeds I will remember no more.

—Hebrews 8:12

If we say that we have no sin, we deceive ourselves, and the truth is not in us. If we confess our sins, He is faithful and just to forgive us our sins and cleanse us from all unrighteousness.

—1 John 1:8–9

FRUSTRATION

Though I walk in the midst of trouble, You will preserve me; You stretch forth Your hand against the wrath of my enemies, and Your right hand saves me. The Lord will fulfill His purpose for me; Your mercy, O Lord, endures forever; do not forsake the works of Your hands.

—Psalm 138:7–8

Every way of a man is right in his own eyes, but the Lord weighs the hearts. To do justice and judgment is more acceptable to the Lord than sacrifice.

—Proverbs 21:2–3

What then shall we say to these things? If God is for us, who can be against us? He who did not spare His own Son, but delivered Him up for us all, how shall He not with Him also freely give us all things?

—Romans 8:31–32

No temptation has taken you except what is common to man. God is faithful, and He will not permit you to be tempted above what you can endure, but will with the temptation also make a way to escape, that you may be able to bear it.

—1 Corinthians 10:13

Let us firmly hold the profession of our faith without wavering, for He who promised is faithful.

—Hebrews 10:23

FULFILLMENT

The Lord is my shepherd; I shall not want. He makes me lie down in green pastures; He leads me beside still waters. He restores my soul; He leads me in paths of righteousness for His name's sake. Even though I walk through the valley of the shadow of death, I will fear no evil; for You are with me; Your rod and Your staff, they comfort me. You prepare a table before me in the presence of my enemies; You anoint my head with oil; my cup runs over. Surely goodness and mercy shall follow me all the days of my life, and I will dwell in the house of the Lord forever.

—Psalm 23:1–6

The eyes of all wait upon You, and You give them their food in due season. You open Your hand and satisfy the desire of every living thing.

—Psalm 145:15–16

While we were yet weak, in due time Christ died for the ungodly. Rarely for a righteous man will one die. Yet perhaps for a good man some would even dare to die. But God demonstrates His own love toward us, in that while we were yet sinners, Christ died for us.

—Romans 5:6–8

"This is the covenant that I will make with them after those days, says the Lord: I will put My laws into their hearts, and in their minds I will write them," then He adds, "Their sins and lawless deeds will I remember no more."

—Hebrews 10:16–17

His divine power has given to us all things that pertain to life and godliness through the knowledge of Him who has called us by His own glory and excellence, by which He has given to us exceedingly great and precious promises, so that through these things you might become partakers of the divine nature and escape the corruption that is in the world through lust.

—2 Peter 1:3–4

GAMBLING

He who loves money will not be satisfied with money; nor he who loves abundance with increase. This also is vanity.

—Ecclesiastes 5:10

No one can serve two masters. For either he will hate the one and love the other, or else he will hold to the one and despise the other. You cannot serve God and money.

—Matthew 6:24

Then He said to them, "Take heed and beware of covetousness. For a man's life does not consist in the abundance of his possessions."

—Luke 12:15

But those who desire to be rich fall into temptation and a snare and into many foolish and harmful lusts, which drown men in ruin and destruction. For the love of money is the root of all evil. While coveting after money, some have strayed from the faith and pierced themselves through with many sorrows.

—1 Timothy 6:9–10

Let your lives be without love of money, and be content with the things you have. For He has said: "I will never leave you, nor forsake you."

—Hebrews 13:5

GENEROSITY

And whoever gives even a cup of cold water to one of these little ones in the name of a disciple, truly I tell you, he shall in no way lose his reward.

—Matthew 10:42

Give, and it will be given to you: Good measure, pressed down, shaken together, and running over will men give unto you. For with the measure you use, it will be measured unto you.

—Luke 6:38

He looked up and saw the rich putting their gifts in the treasury. He also saw a poor widow putting in two mites, and He said, "Truly I tell you, this poor widow has put in more than all of them. For all these out of their abundance have put in their gifts for God. But she out of her poverty has put in all the living she had."

—Luke 21:1–4

In all things I have shown you how, working like this, you must help the weak, remembering the words of the Lord Jesus, how He said, "It is more blessed to give than to receive."

—Acts 20:35

Command those who are rich in this world that they not be conceited, nor trust in uncertain riches, but in the living God, who richly gives us all things to enjoy. Command that they do good, that they be rich in good works, generous, willing to share, and laying up in store for themselves a good foundation for the coming age, so that they may take hold of eternal life.

—1 Timothy 6:17–19

GIFTS FROM GOD

For I would that all men were even as I myself. But every man has his proper gift from God, one after this manner and another after that.

—1 Corinthians 7:7

For by grace you have been saved through faith, and this is not of yourselves. It is the gift of God.

—Ephesians 2:8

Do not neglect the gift that is in you, which was given to you by prophecy, with the laying on of hands by the elders.

—1 Timothy 4:14

Therefore I remind you to stir up the gift of God, which is in you by the laying on of my hands.

—2 Timothy 1:6

Every good gift and every perfect gift is from above and comes down from the Father of lights, with whom is no change or shadow of turning.

—James 1:17

As everyone has received a gift, even so serve one another with it, as good stewards of the manifold grace of God.

—1 Peter 4:10

GIVING

Honor the Lord with your substance, and with the first fruits of all your increase; so your barns will be filled with plenty, and your presses will burst out with new wine.

—Proverbs 3:9–10

Do not withhold good from those to whom it is due, when it is in the power of your hand to do it.

—Proverbs 3:27

Will a man rob God? Yet you have robbed Me. But you say, "How have we robbed You?" In tithes and offerings.

—Malachi 3:8

Bring all the tithes into the storehouse, that there may be food in My house, and test Me now in this, says the Lord of Hosts, if I will not open for you the windows of heaven and pour out for you a blessing, that there will not be room enough to receive it. I will rebuke the devourer for your sakes, so that it will not destroy the fruit of your ground, and the vines in your field will not fail to bear fruit, says the LORD of Hosts.

—MALACHI 3:10–11

And whoever gives even a cup of cold water to one of these little ones in the name of a disciple, truly I tell you, he shall in no way lose his reward.

—MATTHEW 10:42

GOALS

Delight yourself in the LORD, and He will give you the desires of your heart. Commit your way to the LORD; trust also in Him, and He will bring it to pass.

—PSALM 37:4–5

But seek first the kingdom of God and His righteousness, and all these things shall be given to you.

—MATTHEW 6:33

Do you not know that all those who run in a race run, but one receives the prize? So run, that you may obtain it. Everyone who strives for the prize exercises self-control in all things. Now they do it to obtain a corruptible crown, but we an incorruptible one.

—1 CORINTHIANS 9:24–25

So whether present or absent, we labor that we may be accepted by Him.

—2 Corinthians 5:9

And let us not grow weary in doing good, for in due season we shall reap, if we do not give up.

—Galatians 6:9

GOD HEARS OUR PRAYERS

I will bless the Lord at all times; His praise will continually be in my mouth. My soul will make its boast in the Lord; the humble will hear of it and be glad. Oh, magnify the Lord with me, and let us exalt His name together. I sought the Lord, and He answered me, and delivered me from all my fears.

—Psalm 34:1–4

I will abundantly bless her provisions; I will satisfy her poor with bread.

—Psalm 132:15

We know that God does not listen to sinners. But if anyone is a worshipper of God and does His will, He hears him.

—John 9:31

For the eyes of the Lord are on the righteous, and His ears are open to their prayers; but the face of the Lord is against those who do evil.

—1 Peter 3:12

This is the confidence that we have in Him, that if we ask anything according to His will, He hears us. So if we know that He hears whatever we ask, we know that we have whatever we asked of Him.

—1 John 5:14–15

GOD IS ALWAYS WITH YOU

Have not I commanded you? Be strong and courageous. Do not be afraid or dismayed, for the Lord your God is with you wherever you go.

—Joshua 1:9

Is not the Lord your God with you? Has He not given you rest all around? For He has given the inhabitants of the land into my hand, and the land is subdued before the Lord and His people.

—1 Chronicles 22:18

The Lord is my shepherd; I shall not want. He makes me lie down in green pastures; He leads me beside still waters. He restores my soul; He leads me in paths of righteousness for His name's sake. Even though I walk through the valley of the shadow of death, I will fear no evil; for You are with me; Your rod and Your staff, they comfort me.

—Psalm 23:1–4

Do not fear, for I am with you; do not be dismayed, for I am your God. I will strengthen you, I will help you, yes, I will uphold you with My righteous right hand.

—Isaiah 41:10

Let your lives be without love of money, and be content with the things you have. For He has said: "I will never leave you, nor forsake you."

—Hebrews 13:5

GOD'S FAITHFULNESS

God is not a man, that He should lie, nor a son of man, that He should repent. Has He spoken, and will He not do it? Or has He spoken, and will He not make it good?

—Numbers 23:19

Know therefore that the Lord your God, He is God, the faithful God, who keeps covenant and mercy with them who love Him and keep His commandments to a thousand generations.

—Deuteronomy 7:9

My eyes shall be favorable to the faithful in the land, that they may live with me; he who walks in a blameless manner, he shall serve me. He who practices deceit shall not dwell within my house; he who tells lies shall not remain in my sight.

—Psalm 101:6–7

A faithful man will abound with blessings, but he who makes haste to be rich will not be innocent.

—PROVERBS 28:20

Who then is a faithful and wise servant, whom his master has made ruler over his household to give them food at the appointed time? Blessed is that servant whom his master will find so doing when he comes. Truly, I say to you that he will make him ruler over all his goods.

—MATTHEW 24:45–47

Let us firmly hold the profession of our faith without wavering, for He who promised is faithful.

—HEBREWS 10:23

GOD'S FAVOR

May God be gracious to us, and bless us, and cause His face to shine on us; Selah…God will bless us, and all the ends of the earth will fear Him.

—PSALM 67:1, 7

Remember me, O LORD, when You give favor to Your people; visit me with Your deliverance.

—PSALM 106:4

In righteousness you shall be established; you shall be far from oppression, for you shall not fear, and from terror, for it shall not come near you.

—ISAIAH 54:14

For the weapons of our warfare are not carnal, but mighty through God to the pulling down of strongholds.

—2 Corinthians 10:4

Christ has redeemed us from the curse of the law by being made a curse for us—as it is written, "Cursed is everyone who hangs on a tree."

—Galatians 3:13

Blessed be the God and Father of our Lord Jesus Christ, who has blessed us with every spiritual blessing in the heavenly places in Christ.

—Ephesians 1:3

Stand therefore, having your waist girded with truth, having put on the breastplate of righteousness, having your feet fitted with the readiness of the gospel of peace, and above all, taking the shield of faith, with which you will be able to extinguish all the fiery arrows of the evil one. Take the helmet of salvation and the sword of the Spirit, which is the word of God.

—Ephesians 6:14–17

Every good gift and every perfect gift is from above and comes down from the Father of lights, with whom is no change or shadow of turning.

—James 1:17

GOD'S PRESENCE

He shall call upon Me, and I will answer him; I will be with him in trouble, and I will deliver him and honor him. With long life I will satisfy him and show him My salvation.

—Psalm 91:15–16

Where shall I go from Your spirit, or where shall I flee from Your presence? If I ascend to heaven, You are there; if I make my bed in Sheol, You are there. If I take the wings of the morning and dwell at the end of the sea, even there Your hand shall guide me, and Your right hand shall take hold of me.

—Psalm 139:7–10

Do not fear, for I am with you; do not be dismayed, for I am your God. I will strengthen you, I will help you, yes, I will uphold you with My righteous right hand.

—Isaiah 41:10

Draw near to God, and He will draw near to you. Cleanse your hands, you sinners, and purify your hearts, you double-minded.

—James 4:8

No one has seen God at any time. If we love one another, God dwells in us, and His love is perfected in us.

—1 John 4:12

GOD'S PROTECTION

They shall be Mine, says the Lord of Hosts, on the day when I make up My jewels. And I will spare them as a man spares his son who serves him.

—Malachi 3:17

For truly I say to you, whoever says to this mountain, "Be removed and be thrown into the sea," and does not doubt in his heart, but believes that what he says will come to pass, he will have whatever he says. Therefore I say to you, whatever things you ask when you pray, believe that you will receive them, and you will have them.

—Mark 11:23–24

Therefore take up the whole armor of God that you may be able to resist in the evil day, and having done all, to stand.

—Ephesians 6:13

Fight the good fight of faith. Lay hold on eternal life, to which you are called and have professed a good profession before many witnesses.

—1 Timothy 6:12

Therefore submit yourselves to God. Resist the devil, and he will flee from you.

—James 4:7

GOD'S WILL

Delight yourself in the Lord, and He will give you the desires of your heart.

—Psalm 37:4

Trust in the Lord with all your heart, and lean not on your own understanding; in all your ways acknowledge Him, and He will direct your paths.

—Proverbs 3:5–6

But seek first the kingdom of God and His righteousness, and all these things shall be given to you. Therefore, take no thought about tomorrow, for tomorrow will take thought about the things of itself. Sufficient to the day is the trouble thereof.

—Matthew 6:33–34

For God is the One working in you, both to will and to do His good pleasure.

—Philippians 2:13

Rejoice always. Pray without ceasing. In everything give thanks, for this is the will of God in Christ Jesus concerning you.

—1 Thessalonians 5:16–18

GRACE

He does not treat us according to our sins, nor repay us according to our iniquities...as far as the east is from the west, so far has He removed our transgressions from us.

—Psalm 103:10, 12

Let the wicked forsake his way, and the unrighteous man his thoughts; and let him return to the Lord, and He will have mercy upon him, and to our God, for He will abundantly pardon.

—Isaiah 55:7

I press toward the goal to the prize of the high calling of God in Christ Jesus. Therefore let those of us who are mature be thus minded. And if you think differently in any way, God will reveal even this to you. Nevertheless, according to what we have already attained, let us walk by the same rule, let us be of the same mind.

—Philippians 3:14–16

For we do not have a High Priest who cannot sympathize with our weaknesses, but One who was in every sense tempted like we are, yet without sin. Let us then come with confidence to the throne of grace, that we may obtain mercy and find grace to help in time of need.

—Hebrews 4:15–16

Grace and peace be multiplied to you through the knowledge of God and of Jesus our Lord. His divine power has given to us all things that pertain to life and godliness through the knowledge of Him who has called us by His own glory and excellence.

—2 Peter 1:2–3

GRIEF AND DEATH

The eye of the Lord is on those who fear Him, on those who hope in His lovingkindness, to deliver their soul from death, and to keep them alive in famine. Our soul waits for the Lord; He is our help and our shield.

—Psalm 33:18–20

Blessed are those who mourn, for they shall be comforted.

—Matthew 5:4

For I am persuaded that neither death nor life, neither angels nor principalities nor powers, neither things present nor things to come, neither height nor depth, nor any other created thing, shall be able to separate us from the love of God, which is in Christ Jesus our Lord.

—Romans 8:38–39

For none of us lives for himself, and no one dies for himself. For if we live, we live for the Lord. And if we die, we die for the Lord. So, whether we live or die, we are the Lord's.

—Romans 14:7–8

Then I heard a voice from heaven saying to me, "Write: Blessed are the dead who die in the Lord from now on." "Yes," says the Spirit, "that they may rest from their labors, for their works follow them."

—Revelation 14:13

GUIDANCE

When you go, they will lead you; when you sleep, they will keep you; and when you awake, they will speak with you. For the commandment is a lamp, and the law is light; and reproofs of instruction are the way of life.

—Proverbs 6:22–23

Commit your works to the Lord, and your thoughts will be established.

—Proverbs 16:3

Your ears shall hear a word behind you, saying, "This is the way, walk in it," whenever you turn to the right hand and when you turn to the left.

—Isaiah 30:21

But when the Spirit of truth comes, He will guide you into all truth. For He will not speak on His own authority. But He will speak whatever He hears, and He will tell you things that are to come.

—John 16:13

If any of you lacks wisdom, let him ask of God, who gives to all men liberally and without criticism, and it will be given to him.

—James 1:5

GUILT

When I kept silent, my bones wasted away through my groaning all day long....I acknowledged my sin to You, and my iniquity I did not conceal. I said, "I will confess my transgressions to the Lord," and You forgave the iniquity of my sin. Selah.

—Psalm 32:3, 5

For though you wash yourself with lye, and take much soap, yet your iniquity is marked before Me, says the Lord God.

—Jeremiah 2:22

For I will be merciful toward their unrighteousness, and their sins and their lawless deeds I will remember no more.

—Hebrews 8:12

For whoever shall keep the whole law and yet offend in one point is guilty of breaking the whole law.

—James 2:10

But if we walk in the light as He is in the light, we have fellowship one with another, and the blood of Jesus Christ His Son cleanses us from all sin.

—1 John 1:7

HABITS

Put away from you a deceitful mouth, and put perverse lips far from you. Let your eyes look right on, and let your eyelids look straight before you. Ponder the path of your feet, and let all your ways be established. Do not turn to the right or to the left; remove your foot from evil.

—Proverbs 4:24–27

Do not be conformed to this world, but be transformed by the renewing of your mind, that you may prove what is the good and acceptable and perfect will of God.

—Romans 12:2

"All things are lawful to me," but not all things are helpful. "All things are lawful for me," but I will not be brought under the power of anything.

—1 Corinthians 6:12

No temptation has taken you except what is common to man. God is faithful, and He will not permit you to be tempted above what you can endure, but will with the temptation also make a way to escape, that you may be able to bear it.

—1 Corinthians 10:13

Therefore be imitators of God as beloved children.

—Ephesians 5:1

HEALING

Do not be wise in your own eyes; fear the Lord and depart from evil. It will be health to your body, and strength to your bones.

—Proverbs 3:7–8

Then you shall call, and the Lord shall answer; you shall cry, and He shall say, Here I am. If you take away the yoke from your midst, the pointing of the finger, and speaking wickedness.

—Isaiah 58:9

I will bring it health and healing, and I will heal them; and I will reveal to them the abundance of peace and truth.

—Jeremiah 33:6

Jesus answered them, "Have faith in God. For truly I say to you, whoever says to this mountain, 'Be removed and be thrown into the sea,' and does not doubt in his heart, but believes that what he says will come to pass, he will have whatever he says. Therefore I say to you, whatever things you ask when you pray, believe that you will receive them, and you will have them.

—Mark 11:22–24

And whatever we ask, we will receive from Him, because we keep His commandments and do the things that are pleasing in His sight. And this is His commandment: that we should believe on the name of His Son Jesus Christ and love one another as He commanded us.

—1 John 3:22–23

HELP IN TROUBLES

Cast your burden on the LORD, and He will sustain you; He will never allow the righteous to be moved.

—PSALM 55:22

You who have shown me great distresses and troubles will revive me again, and will bring me up again from the depths of the earth.

—PSALM 71:20

There shall be no evil befall you, neither shall any plague come near your tent; for He shall give His angels charge over you to guard you in all your ways.

—PSALM 91:10–11

For the Lord will not cast off forever. But though He causes grief, yet He will have compassion according to the abundance of His mercies. For He does not afflict from His heart, nor grieve the sons of men.

—LAMENTATIONS 3:31–33

The LORD is good, a stronghold in the day of distress; and He knows those who take refuge in Him.

—NAHUM 1:7

HOLINESS

I urge you therefore, brothers, by the mercies of God, that you present your bodies as a living sacrifice, holy, and acceptable to

God, which is your reasonable service of worship. Do not be conformed to this world, but be transformed by the renewing of your mind, that you may prove what is the good and acceptable and perfect will of God.

—Romans 12:1–2

Just as He chose us in Him before the foundation of the world, to be holy and blameless before Him in love.

—Ephesians 1:4

Finally, brothers, whatever things are true, whatever things are honest, whatever things are just, whatever things are pure, whatever things are lovely, whatever things are of good report, if there is any virtue, and if there is any praise, think on these things.

—Philippians 4:8

But as He who has called you is holy, so be holy in all your conduct, Because it is written, "Be holy, for I am holy."

—1 Peter 1:15–16

His divine power has given to us all things that pertain to life and godliness through the knowledge of Him who has called us by His own glory and excellence.

—2 Peter 1:3

HOLY SPIRIT

As for Me, this is My covenant with them, says the Lord: My Spirit who is upon you, and My words which I have put in your mouth shall not depart out of your mouth, nor out of the mouth of your descendants, nor out of the mouth of your descendants' descendants, says the LORD, from this time forth and forever.

—ISAIAH 59:21

But the Counselor, the Holy Spirit, whom the Father will send in My name, will teach you everything and remind you of all that I told you.

—JOHN 14:26

Likewise, the Spirit helps us in our weaknesses, for we do not know what to pray for as we ought, but the Spirit Himself intercedes for us with groanings too deep for words. He who searches the hearts knows what the mind of the Spirit is, because He intercedes for the saints according to the will of God.

—ROMANS 8:26–27

For the kingdom of God does not mean eating and drinking, but righteousness and peace and joy in the Holy Spirit.

—ROMANS 14:17

So that the blessing of Abraham might come on the Gentiles through Jesus Christ, that we might receive the promise of the Spirit through faith.

—GALATIANS 3:14

HONESTY

Do not lie one to another, since you have put off the old nature with its deeds, and have embraced the new nature, which is renewed in knowledge after the image of Him who created it.

—Colossians 3:9–10

And that no man take advantage of and defraud his brother in any matter, because the Lord is the avenger in all these things, as we also have forewarned you and testified. For God has not called us to uncleanness, but to holiness.

—1 Thessalonians 4:6–7

In all things presenting yourself as an example of good works: in doctrine showing integrity, gravity, incorruptibility, and sound speech that cannot be condemned, so that the one who opposes you may be ashamed, having nothing evil to say of you.

—Titus 2:7–8

Pray for us. For we trust that we have a good conscience and in all things are willing to live honestly.

—Hebrews 13:18

Live your lives honorably among the Gentiles, so that though they speak against you as evildoers, they shall see your good works and thereby glorify God in the day of visitation.

—1 Peter 2:12

HOPE

The eye of the Lord is on those who fear Him, on those who hope in His lovingkindness.

—Psalm 33:18

For You are my hope, O Lord God; You are my confidence from my youth.

—Psalm 71:5

So shall the knowledge of wisdom be to your soul; when you have found it, then there will be a reward, and your expectation will not be cut off.

—Proverbs 24:14

Blessed is the man who trusts in the Lord, and whose hope is the Lord. For he shall be as a tree planted by the waters, and that spreads out its roots by the river, and shall not fear when heat comes, but its leaf shall be green, and it shall not be anxious in the year of drought, neither shall cease from yielding fruit.

—Jeremiah 17:7–8

"The Lord is my portion," says my soul, "therefore I will hope in Him." The Lord is good to those who wait for Him, to the soul who seeks Him.

—Lamentations 3:24–25

Therefore my heart was glad, and my tongue rejoiced; moreover my flesh will dwell in hope. For You will not abandon my soul to Hades, nor will You allow Your Holy One to see corruption. You have made known to me the ways of life; You will make me full of joy with Your presence.

—Acts 2:26–28

HOW TO BE BORN AGAIN

For God did not send His Son into the world to condemn the world, but that the world through Him might be saved. He who believes in Him is not condemned. But he who does not believe is condemned already, because he has not believed in the name of the only begotten Son of God.

—John 3:17–18

He then led them out and asked, "Sirs, what must I do to be saved?" They said, "Believe in the Lord Jesus Christ, and you and your household will be saved."

—Acts 16:30–31

For I delivered to you first of all that which I also received: how Christ died for our sins according to the Scriptures, was buried, rose again the third day according to the Scriptures.

—1 Corinthians 15:3–4

But God, being rich in mercy, because of His great love with which He loved us, even when we were dead in sins, made us alive together with Christ (by grace you have been saved)....For by grace you have been saved through faith, and this is not of yourselves. It is the gift of God, not of works, so that no one should boast.

—Ephesians 2:4–9

He Himself bore our sins in His own body on the tree, that we, being dead to sins, should live unto righteousness. "By His wounds you were healed."

—1 Peter 2:24

HUMILITY

If My people, who are called by My name, will humble themselves and pray, and seek My face and turn from their wicked ways, then I will hear from heaven, and will forgive their sin and will heal their land.

—2 Chronicles 7:14

The desire of the humble You have heard, O Lord; You make their heart attentive; You bend Your ear.

—Psalm 10:17

A man's pride will bring him low, but honor will uphold the humble in spirit.

—Proverbs 29:23

Therefore whoever humbles himself like this little child is greatest in the kingdom of heaven.

—Matthew 18:4

Let this mind be in you all, which was also in Christ Jesus, who, being in the form of God, did not consider equality with God something to be grasped. But He emptied Himself, taking upon Himself the form of a servant, and was made in the likeness of men. And being found in the form of a man, He humbled Himself and became obedient to death, even death on a cross.

—Philippians 2:5–8

HUSBANDS

Enjoy life with the wife whom you love all the days of your vain life which He has given you under the sun; because that is your reward in life and in your toil because you have labored under the sun.

—Ecclesiastes 9:9

In this way men ought to love their wives as their own bodies. He who loves his wife loves himself.

—Ephesians 5:28

Husbands, love your wives, and do not be bitter toward them.

—Colossians 3:19

But if any do not care for their own, and especially for those of their own house, they have denied the faith and are worse than unbelievers.

—1 Timothy 5:8

Likewise, you husbands, live considerately with your wives, giving honor to the woman as the weaker vessel, since they too are also heirs of the grace of life, so that your prayers will not be hindered.

—1 Peter 3:7

HYPOCRISY

Therefore, the Lord said: Because this people draw near with their mouths and honor Me with their lips, but have removed their hearts far from Me, and their fear toward Me is tradition by the precept of men.

—Isaiah 29:13

You hypocrite! First take the plank out of your own eye, and then you will see clearly to take the speck out of your brother's eye.

—Matthew 7:5

Woe to you, scribes and Pharisees, hypocrites! You are like whitewashed tombs, which indeed appear beautiful outwardly, but inside are full of dead men's bones and of all uncleanness. So you also outwardly appear righteous to men, but inside you are full of hypocrisy and iniquity.

—Matthew 23:27–28

If anyone among you seems to be religious and does not bridle his tongue, but deceives his own heart, this man's religion is vain.

—James 1:26

If anyone says, "I love God," and hates his brother, he is a liar. For whoever does not love his brother whom he has seen, how can he love God whom he has not seen?

—1 John 4:20

INHERITANCE

The righteous will inherit the land, and dwell on it forever.

—Psalm 37:29

An inheritance may be gained hastily at the beginning, but the end of it will not be blessed.

—Proverbs 20:21

Therefore you are no longer a servant, but a son, and if a son, then an heir of God through Christ.

—Galatians 4:7

That the eyes of your understanding may be enlightened, that you may know what is the hope of His calling and what are the riches of the glory of His inheritance among the saints.

—Ephesians 1:18

Servants, obey your masters in all things according to the flesh, serving not only when they are watching, as the servants of men, but in singleness of heart, fearing God. And whatever you do, do it heartily, as for the Lord and not for men.

—Colossians 3:22–23

By which He has given to us exceedingly great and precious promises, so that through these things you might become partakers of the divine nature and escape the corruption that is in the world through lust.

—2 Peter 1:4

INTEGRITY

The integrity of the upright will guide them, but the perverseness of transgressors will destroy them.

—Proverbs 11:3

Learn to be calm, and to conduct your own business, and to work with your own hands, as we commanded you, so that you may walk honestly toward those who are outsiders and that you may lack nothing.

—1 Thessalonians 4:11–12

In all things presenting yourself as an example of good works: in doctrine showing integrity, gravity, incorruptibility, and sound speech that cannot be condemned, so that the one who opposes you may be ashamed, having nothing evil to say of you.

—Titus 2:7–8

Pray for us. For we trust that we have a good conscience and in all things are willing to live honestly.

—Hebrews 13:18

Live your lives honorably among the Gentiles, so that though they speak against you as evildoers, they shall see your good works and thereby glorify God in the day of visitation.

—1 Peter 2:12

JESUS CHRIST

For God so loved the world that He gave His only begotten Son, that whoever believes in Him should not perish, but have eternal life. For God did not send His Son into the world to condemn the world, but that the world through Him might be saved.

—John 3:16–17

For none of us lives for himself, and no one dies for himself. For if we live, we live for the Lord. And if we die, we die for the Lord. So, whether we live or die, we are the Lord's.

—Romans 14:7–8

He is the brightness of His glory, the express image of Himself, and upholds all things by the word of His power. When He had by Himself purged our sins, He sat down at the right hand of the Majesty on high.

—Hebrews 1:3

So that by two immutable things, in which it was impossible for God to lie, we who have fled for refuge might have strong encouragement to hold fast to the hope set before us. We have this hope as a sure and steadfast anchor of the soul, which enters the Inner Place behind the veil.

—Hebrews 6:18–19

And we have seen and testify that the Father sent the Son to be the Savior of the world.

—1 John 4:14

JUDGING OTHERS

Judge not, and you shall not be judged. Condemn not, and you will not be condemned. Forgive, and you shall be forgiven.

—Luke 6:37

So when they continued asking Him, He stood up and said to them, "Let him who is without sin among you be the first to throw a stone at her."

—John 8:7

Therefore you are without excuse, O man, whoever you are who judges, for when you judge another, you condemn yourself, for you who judge do the same things. But we know that the judgment of God is according to truth against those who commit such things. Do you think, O man, who judges those who do such things, and who does the same thing, that you will escape the judgment of God?

—Romans 2:1–3

Let no unwholesome word proceed out of your mouth, but only that which is good for building up, that it may give grace to the listeners.

—Ephesians 4:29

Do not speak evil of one another, brothers. He who speaks evil of his brother and judges his brother speaks evil of the law and judges the law. If you judge the law, you are not a doer of the law, but a judge. There is one Lawgiver who is able to save and to destroy. Who are you to judge another?

—James 4:11–12

JUSTICE

It is joy to the just to do justice, but destruction will come to the workers of iniquity.

—Proverbs 21:15

Therefore, the Lord longs to be gracious to you, and therefore, He waits on high to have mercy on you; for the Lord is a God of justice; how blessed are all who long for Him.

—Isaiah 30:18

But let justice roll down like water, and righteousness like an ever-flowing stream.

—Amos 5:24

He has told you, O man, what is good—and what does the LORD require of you, but to do justice and to love kindness, and to walk humbly with your God?

—MICAH 6:8

Beloved, do not avenge yourselves, but rather give place to God's wrath, for it is written: "Vengeance is Mine. I will repay," says the Lord.

—ROMANS 12:19

KINDNESS

A good man shows generous favor, and lends; he will guide his affairs with justice.

—PSALM 112:5

Heaviness in the heart of man makes it droop, but a good word makes it glad.

—PROVERBS 12:25

But let him who glories glory in this, that he understands and knows Me, that I am the LORD who exercises lovingkindness, justice, and righteousness in the earth. For in these things I delight, says the LORD.

—JEREMIAH 9:24

Thus says the LORD of Hosts: Execute true justice, show mercy and compassion, every man to his brother.

—ZECHARIAH 7:9

And whoever gives even a cup of cold water to one of these little ones in the name of a disciple, truly I tell you, he shall in no way lose his reward.

—Matthew 10:42

KNOWLEDGE

When wisdom enters your heart, and knowledge is pleasant to your soul.

—Proverbs 2:10

The heart of the prudent gets knowledge, and the ear of the wise seeks knowledge.

—Proverbs 18:15

The Spirit of the Lord shall rest upon him, the Spirit of wisdom and understanding, the Spirit of counsel and might, the Spirit of knowledge and of the fear of the Lord.

—Isaiah 11:2

My people are destroyed for lack of knowledge. Because you have rejected knowledge, I will reject you from being My priest. And because you have forgotten the law of your God, I will also forget your children. As they increased, so they sinned against Me. I will change their glory into shame.

—Hosea 4:6–7

For this reason we also, since the day we heard it, do not cease to pray for you and to ask that you may be filled with the knowledge of His will in all wisdom and spiritual understanding.

—COLOSSIANS 1:9

LAZINESS

He becomes poor who deals with a slack hand, but the hand of the diligent makes rich. He who gathers in summer is a wise son, but he who sleeps in harvest is a son who causes shame.

—PROVERBS 10:4–5

Learn to be calm, and to conduct your own business, and to work with your own hands, as we commanded you, so that you may walk honestly toward those who are outsiders and that you may lack nothing.

—1 THESSALONIANS 4:11–12

For when we were with you, we commanded you that if any will not work, neither shall he eat. For we hear that there are some among you who live in idleness, mere busybodies, not working at all. Now, concerning those who are such, we command and exhort by our Lord Jesus Christ that they quietly work and eat their own bread.

—2 THESSALONIANS 3:10–12

Besides that, they learn to be idle, and not only idle, wandering around from house to house, but also gossips and busybodies, saying what they ought not.

—1 Timothy 5:13

So that you may not be lazy, but imitators of those who through faith and patience inherit the promises.

—Hebrews 6:12

LEADERSHIP

But Jesus called them to Him and said, "You know that the rulers of the Gentiles lord it over them, and those who are great exercise authority over them. It shall not be so among you. Whoever would be great among you, let him serve you, and whoever would be first among you, let him be your slave, even as the Son of Man did not come to be served, but to serve and to give His life as a ransom for many."

—Matthew 20:25–28

But Jesus called them together, and said, "You know that those who are appointed to rule over the Gentiles lord it over them, and their great ones exercise authority over them. But it shall not be so among you. Whoever would be great among you must be your servant, and whoever among you would be greatest must be servant of all. For even the Son of Man came not to be served, but to serve, and to give His life as a ransom for many."

—Mark 10:42–45

So when He had washed their feet, and put on His garments, and sat down again, He said to them, "Do you know what I have done to you? You call Me Teacher and Lord. You speak accurately, for so I am. If I then, your Lord and Teacher, have washed your feet, you also ought to wash one another's feet. For I have given you an example, that you should do as I have done to you."

—John 13:12–15

Let love be without hypocrisy. Hate what is evil. Cleave to what is good. Be devoted to one another with brotherly love; prefer one another in honor, do not be lazy in diligence, be fervent in spirit, serve the Lord, rejoice in hope, be patient in suffering, persevere in prayer, contribute to the needs of the saints, practice hospitality.

—Romans 12:9–13

Let nothing be done out of strife or conceit, but in humility let each esteem the other better than himself.

—Philippians 2:3

LISTENING

So that you incline your ear to wisdom, and apply your heart to understanding.

—Proverbs 2:2

He who answers a matter before he hears it, it is folly and shame to him.

—Proverbs 18:13

Hear counsel and receive instruction, that you may be wise in your latter days.

—Proverbs 19:20

He who is of God hears God's words. Therefore, you do not hear them, because you are not of God.

—John 8:47

Therefore, my beloved brothers, let every man be swift to hear, slow to speak, and slow to anger.

—James 1:19

He who has an ear, let him hear what the Spirit says to the churches. To him who overcomes I will give permission to eat of the tree of life, which is in the midst of the Paradise of God.

—Revelation 2:7

LONG LIFE

So that you might fear the Lord your God in order to keep all His statutes and His commandments which I command you—you, and your son, and your grandson—all the days of your life, so that your days may be prolonged.

—Deuteronomy 6:2

Do not cast me off in the time of old age; do not forsake me when my strength fails.

—Psalm 71:9

With long life I will satisfy him and show him My salvation.

—Psalm 91:16

My son, do not forget my teaching, but let your heart keep my commandments; for length of days and long life and peace will they add to you.

—Proverbs 3:1–2

The fear of the Lord prolongs days, but the years of the wicked will be shortened.

—Proverbs 10:27

LOVE

You shall not take vengeance, nor bear any grudge against the children of your people, but you shall love your neighbor as yourself: I am the Lord.

—Leviticus 19:18

Know therefore that the Lord your God, He is God, the faithful God, who keeps covenant and mercy with them who love Him and keep His commandments to a thousand generations.

—Deuteronomy 7:9

I love those who love me, and those who seek me early will find me.

—Proverbs 8:17

Walk in love, as Christ loved us and gave Himself for us as a fragrant offering and a sacrifice to God.

—Ephesians 5:2

As concerning brotherly love, you do not need me to write to you. For you yourselves are taught by God to love one another.

—1 Thessalonians 4:9

LOVE ONE ANOTHER

Behold, how good and how pleasant it is for brothers to dwell together in unity!

—Psalm 133:1

A new commandment I give to you, that you love one another, even as I have loved you, that you also love one another. By this all men will know that you are My disciples, if you have love for one another.

—John 13:34–35

As concerning brotherly love, you do not need me to write to you. For you yourselves are taught by God to love one another.

—1 Thessalonians 4:9

If you fulfill the royal law according to the Scripture, "You shall love your neighbor as yourself," you are doing well.

—James 2:8

Since your souls have been purified by obedience to the truth through the Spirit unto a genuine brotherly love, love one another deeply with a pure heart.

—1 Peter 1:22

LOVING GOD

Know therefore that the Lord your God, He is God, the faithful God, who keeps covenant and mercy with them who love Him and keep His commandments to a thousand generations.

—Deuteronomy 7:9

Because he has set his love upon Me, therefore I will deliver him; I will set him on high, because he has known My name.

—Psalm 91:14

The Lord preserves all those who love Him, but all the wicked He will destroy.

—Psalm 145:20

If you keep My commandments, you will remain in My love, even as I have kept My Father's commandments and remain in His love.

—John 15:10

But as it is written, "Eye has not seen, nor ear heard, neither has it entered into the heart of man, the things which God has prepared for those who love Him."

—1 Corinthians 2:9

LOYALTY

But Ruth said, "Do not urge me to leave you or to turn back from following you. For wherever you go, I will go, and wherever you stay, I will stay. Your people shall be my people and your God my God. Where you die, I will die, and there I will be buried. May the Lord do thus to me, and worse, if anything but death separates you and me!"

—Ruth 1:16–17

O Lord, the God of Abraham, Isaac, and Israel, our fathers, keep this forever in the thoughts and intentions of the heart of Your people and direct their heart to You.

—1 Chronicles 29:18

That they might set their hope in God and not forget the works of God, but keep His commandments, and they might not be as their fathers, a stubborn and rebellious generation, a generation that did not set their heart steadfast, and whose spirit was not faithful to God.

—Psalm 78:7–8

A man who has friends must show himself friendly, and there is a friend who sticks closer than a brother.

—Proverbs 18:24

If it be so, our God whom we serve is able to deliver us from the burning fiery furnace, and He will deliver us out of your hand, O king. But even if He does not, be it known to you, O king, that we will not serve your gods, nor worship the golden image which you have set up.

—Daniel 3:17–18

LUST

Do not lust after her beauty in your heart, nor let her allure you with her eyelids. For by means of a harlot a man is reduced to a piece of bread, and the adulteress will prey upon his precious life. Can a man take fire in his bosom, and his clothes not be burned? Can one walk upon hot coals, and his feet not be burned? So he who goes in to his neighbor's wife; whoever touches her will not be innocent.

—Proverbs 6:25–29

Likewise, you also consider yourselves to be dead to sin, but alive to God through Jesus Christ our Lord. Therefore do not let sin reign in your mortal body, that you should obey it in its lusts…For sin shall not have dominion over you, for you are not under the law, but under grace.

—Romans 6:11–14

Let no man say when he is tempted, "I am tempted by God," for God cannot be tempted with evil; neither does He tempt anyone.

—James 1:13

Therefore submit yourselves to God. Resist the devil, and he will flee from you. Draw near to God, and He will draw near to you. Cleanse your hands, you sinners, and purify your hearts, you double-minded.

—James 4:7–8

Dearly beloved, I implore you as aliens and refugees, abstain from fleshly lusts, which wage war against the soul.

—1 Peter 2:11

LYING

You must not give a false report. Do not join your hand with the wicked to be a malicious witness.

—Exodus 23:1

You shall not swear falsely by My name, and so defile the name of your God: I am the Lord.

—Leviticus 19:12

If a false witness rises up against any man to testify against him to accuse him of doing wrong, then both the men between whom the controversy is must stand before the Lord, before the priests and the judges, who are in office those days. The judges will thoroughly investigate, and if the witness is a false witness and has testified falsely against his brother, then you must do to him as he conspired to have done to his brother. In this way you must remove the evil from among you.

—Deuteronomy 19:16–19

The truthful lip will be established forever, but a lying tongue is but for a moment.

—Proverbs 12:19

Do not be a witness against your neighbor without cause, and do not deceive with your lips.

—Proverbs 24:28

MANHOOD

You have given him dominion over the works of Your hands; You have put all things under his feet, all sheep and oxen, and also the beasts of the field, the birds of the air, and the fish of the sea, and whatever travels the paths of the seas. O Lord, our Lord, how excellent is Your name in all the earth!

—Psalm 8:6–9

A man's heart devises his way, but the Lord directs his steps.

—Proverbs 16:9

But now, O Lord, You are our Father; we are the clay, and You are our potter; and we all are the work of Your hand.

—Isaiah 64:8

He has told you, O man, what is good—and what does the Lord require of you, but to do justice and to love kindness, and to walk humbly with your God?

—Micah 6:8

Watch, stand fast in the faith, be bold like men, and be strong. Let all that you do be done with love.

—1 Corinthians 16:13–14

MARRIAGE

Let your fountain be blessed, and rejoice with the wife of your youth. Let her be as the loving deer and pleasant doe; let her breasts satisfy you at all times; and always be enraptured with her love. Why should you, my son, be intoxicated by an immoral woman, and embrace the bosom of a seductress?

—Proverbs 5:18–20

Whoever finds a wife finds a good thing, and obtains favor of the Lord.

—Proverbs 18:22

In this way men ought to love their wives as their own bodies. He who loves his wife loves himself.

—Ephesians 5:28

Marriage is to be honored among everyone, and the bed undefiled. But God will judge the sexually immoral and adulterers.

—Hebrews 13:4

Likewise, you husbands, live considerately with your wives, giving honor to the woman as the weaker vessel, since they too are also heirs of the grace of life, so that your prayers will not be hindered.

—1 Peter 3:7

MATERIALISM

Then I turned to all the work that my hands had designed and all the labor that I had toiled to make; and notice, all of it was vanity and chasing the wind. And there was no benefit under the sun.

—Ecclesiastes 2:11

The Pharisees, who were lovers of money, heard all these things and derided Him. He said to them, "You are those who justify yourselves before men, but God knows your hearts. For that which is highly esteemed before men is an abomination before God."

—Luke 16:14–15

But those who desire to be rich fall into temptation and a snare and into many foolish and harmful lusts, which drown men in ruin and destruction. For the love of money is the root of all evil. While coveting after money, some have strayed from the faith and pierced themselves through with many sorrows.

—1 Timothy 6:9–10

For all that is in the world—the lust of the flesh, the lust of the eyes, and the pride of life—is not of the Father, but is of the world.

—1 John 2:16

Whoever has the world's goods and sees his brother in need, but closes his heart of compassion from him, how can the love of God remain in him?

—1 John 3:17

MEEKNESS

The meek will eat and be satisfied; those who seek Him will praise the Lord. May your hearts live forever.

—Psalm 22:26

The meek also shall increase their joy in the Lord, and the poor among men shall rejoice in the Holy One of Israel.

—Isaiah 29:19

Blessed are the meek, for they shall inherit the earth.

—Matthew 5:5

To speak evil of no one, not to be contentious, but gentle, showing all humility toward everyone.

—Titus 3:2

But let it be the hidden nature of the heart, that which is not corruptible, even the ornament of a gentle and quiet spirit, which is very precious in the sight of God.

—1 Peter 3:4

MERCY

(For the Lord your God is a merciful God), He will not abandon you or destroy you or forget the covenant of your fathers which He swore to them.

—Deuteronomy 4:31

David replied to Gad, "I am in great distress. Let me fall into the hands of the Lord, for His mercies are very great, but do not let me fall into the hand of man."

—1 Chronicles 21:13

Like a father shows compassion to his children, so the Lord gives compassion to those who fear Him.

—Psalm 103:13

He prayed to the Lord and said, "O Lord! Is this not what I said while I was still in my own land? This is the reason that I fled before to Tarshish, because I knew that You are a gracious God and merciful, slow to anger, abundant in faithfulness, and ready to relent from punishment."

—Jonah 4:2

Be therefore merciful, even as your Father is merciful.

—Luke 6:36

MONEY

But you must remember the LORD your God, for it is He who gives you the ability to get wealth, so that He may establish His covenant which He swore to your fathers, as it is today.

—DEUTERONOMY 8:18

He who is faithful in what is least is faithful also in much. And he who is dishonest in the least is dishonest also in much. So if you have not been faithful in the unrighteous wealth, who will commit to your trust the true riches?

—LUKE 16:10–11

For the love of money is the root of all evil. While coveting after money, some have strayed from the faith and pierced themselves through with many sorrows.

—1 TIMOTHY 6:10

Let your lives be without love of money, and be content with the things you have. For He has said: "I will never leave you, nor forsake you."

—HEBREWS 13:5

Listen, my beloved brothers. Has God not chosen the poor of this world to be rich in faith and heirs of the kingdom which He has promised to those who love Him?

—JAMES 2:5

MOTIVES

Every way of a man is right in his own eyes, but the Lord weighs the hearts.

—Proverbs 21:2

Therefore judge nothing before the appointed time until the Lord comes. He will bring to light the hidden things of darkness and will reveal the purposes of the hearts. Then everyone will have commendation from God.

—1 Corinthians 4:5

For am I now seeking the approval of men or of God? Or am I trying to please men? For if I were still trying to please men, I would not be the servant of Christ.

—Galatians 1:10

Let nothing be done out of strife or conceit, but in humility let each esteem the other better than himself.

—Philippians 2:3

But as we were allowed by God to be entrusted with the gospel, even so we speak, not to please men, but God, who examines our hearts.

—1 Thessalonians 2:4

MY CALLING

You are the salt of the earth. But if the salt loses its saltiness, how shall it be made salty? It is from then on good for nothing but to be thrown out and to be trampled underfoot by men. You are the light of the world. A city that is set on a hill cannot be hidden

—Matthew 5:13–14

Teaching them to observe all things I have commanded you. And remember, I am with you always, even to the end of the age.
—Matthew 28:20

Truly, truly I say to you, he who believes in Me will do the works that I do also. And he will do greater works than these, because I am going to My Father.

—John 14:12

God is faithful, and by Him you were called to the fellowship of His Son, Jesus Christ our Lord.

—1 Corinthians 1:9

For by grace you have been saved through faith, and this is not of yourselves. It is the gift of God, not of works, so that no one should boast. For we are His workmanship, created in Christ Jesus for good works, which God prepared beforehand, so that we should walk in them.

—Ephesians 2:8–10

For God has not called us to uncleanness, but to holiness.
—1 Thessalonians 4:7

NEED CONFIDENCE

Every way of a man is right in his own eyes, but the Lord weighs the hearts.

—Proverbs 21:2

Therefore judge nothing before the appointed time until the Lord comes. He will bring to light the hidden things of darkness and will reveal the purposes of the hearts. Then everyone will have commendation from God.

—1 Corinthians 4:5

For am I now seeking the approval of men or of God? Or am I trying to please men? For if I were still trying to please men, I would not be the servant of Christ.

—Galatians 1:10

Let nothing be done out of strife or conceit, but in humility let each esteem the other better than himself.

—Philippians 2:3

But as we were allowed by God to be entrusted with the gospel, even so we speak, not to please men, but God, who examines our hearts.

—1 Thessalonians 2:4

NEED COURAGE

Have not I commanded you? Be strong and courageous. Do not be afraid or dismayed, for the Lord your God is with you wherever you go.

—Joshua 1:9

Then David said to Solomon his son, "Be strong and courageous, and take action. Do not be afraid nor be dismayed for the Lord God, my God, is with you. He will not leave you nor forsake you, until you have finished all the work of the service of the house of the Lord."

—1 Chronicles 28:20

Watch, stand fast in the faith, be bold like men, and be strong.

—1 Corinthians 16:13

Do not be frightened by your adversaries. This is a sign to them of their destruction, but of your salvation, and this from God.

—Philippians 1:28

For God has not given us the spirit of fear, but of power, and love, and self-control.

—2 Timothy 1:7

OBEDIENCE

Therefore, keep the words of this covenant and do them, so that you may prosper in all you do.

—Deuteronomy 29:9

Not everyone who says to Me, "Lord, Lord," shall enter the kingdom of heaven, but he who does the will of My Father who is in heaven.

—Matthew 7:21

For whoever does the will of My Father who is in heaven is My brother, and sister, and mother.

—Matthew 12:50

Be doers of the word and not hearers only, deceiving yourselves.

—James 1:22

And whatever we ask, we will receive from Him, because we keep His commandments and do the things that are pleasing in His sight.

—1 John 3:22

OPPRESSION

I have done what is right and just; do not abandon me to my oppressors. Be true to Your servant for good; let not the proud ones oppress me.

—Psalm 119:121–122

For oppression brings confusion to the wise man, and a bribe destroys a man's heart.

—Ecclesiastes 7:7

In righteousness you shall be established; you shall be far from oppression, for you shall not fear, and from terror, for it shall not come near you.

—Isaiah 54:14

Moreover the prince shall not take of the people's inheritance by oppression to thrust them out of their possession. But he shall give his sons inheritance out of his own possession so that My people not be scattered, every man from his possession.

—Ezekiel 46:18

Then I will make camp at My house with a garrison, so that no one can pass back and forth. And no oppressor will pass through them, for now I see with My eyes.

—Zechariah 9:8

OVERWHELMED

The righteous cry out, and the Lord hears, and delivers them out of all their troubles. The Lord is near to the broken-hearted, and saves the contrite of spirit. Many are the afflictions of the righteous, but the Lord delivers him out of them all. A righteous one keeps all his bones; not one of them is broken.

—Psalm 34:17–20

Do not fret because of evildoers, nor be jealous of those who do injustice. For they will quickly wither like the grass, and fade like the green herbs. Trust in the Lord, and do good;

dwell in the land, and practice faithfulness. Delight yourself in the LORD, and He will give you the desires of your heart.

—PSALM 37:1–4

But Jesus looked at them and said, "With men this is impossible, but with God all things are possible."

—MATTHEW 19:26

But when the Spirit of truth comes, He will guide you into all truth. For He will not speak on His own authority. But He will speak whatever He hears, and He will tell you things that are to come.

—JOHN 16:13

But He said to me, "My grace is sufficient for you, for My strength is made perfect in weakness." Therefore most gladly I will boast in my weaknesses, that the power of Christ may rest upon me.

—2 CORINTHIANS 12:9

PARENTING

You shall declare to your son on that day, saying, "This is done because of that which the LORD did for me when I came forth out of Egypt."

—EXODUS 13:8

You shall teach them to your children, speaking of them when you sit in your house and when you walk by the way, when you lie down, and when you rise up.

—Deuteronomy 11:19

The father of the righteous will greatly rejoice, and he who fathers a wise child will have joy of him.

—Proverbs 23:24

Whoever robs his father or his mother and says, "It is no transgression," the same is the companion of a destroyer.

—Proverbs 28:24

Fathers, do not provoke your children to anger, but bring them up in the discipline and instruction of the Lord.

—Ephesians 6:4

PATIENCE

Rest in the Lord, and wait patiently for Him; do not fret because of those who prosper in their way, because of those who make wicked schemes.

—Psalm 37:7

And let us not grow weary in doing good, for in due season we shall reap, if we do not give up.

—Galatians 6:9

Now we exhort you, brothers, warn those who are unruly, comfort the faint-hearted, support the weak, and be patient toward everyone. See that no one renders evil for evil to anyone. But always seek to do good to one another and to all.

—1 Thessalonians 5:14–5

For you need patience, so that after you have done the will of God, you will receive the promise.

—Hebrews 10:36

My brothers, count it all joy when you fall into diverse temptations, knowing that the trying of your faith develops patience. But let patience perfect its work, that you may be perfect and complete, lacking nothing.

—James 1:2–4

PEACE

Now acquaint yourself with Him and be at peace; thereby good will come to you.

—Job 22:21

Mark the blameless man, and consider the upright, for the end of that man is peace.

—Psalm 37:37

The work of righteousness shall be peace, and the effect of righteousness, quietness and assurance forever.

—Isaiah 32:17

I have told you these things so that in Me you may have peace. In the world you will have tribulation. But be of good cheer. I have overcome the world.

—John 16:33

And the peace of God, which surpasses all understanding, will protect your hearts and minds through Christ Jesus.

—Philippians 4:7

PERSEVERANCE IN ADVERSITY

Though I walk in the midst of trouble, You will preserve me; You stretch forth Your hand against the wrath of my enemies, and Your right hand saves me.

—Psalm 138:7

When you pass through waters, I will be with you. And through the rivers, they shall not overflow you. When you walk through the fire, you shall not be burned, nor shall the flame kindle on you.

—Isaiah 43:2

See, I have refined you, but not with silver; I have chosen you in the furnace of affliction.

—Isaiah 48:10

We know that all things work together for good to those who love God, to those who are called according to His purpose.

—Romans 8:28

So that you may not be lazy, but imitators of those who through faith and patience inherit the promises.

—Hebrews 6:12

PERSPECTIVE

But the Lord said to Samuel, "Do not look on his appearance or on the height of his stature, because I have rejected him. For the Lord sees not as man sees. For man looks on the outward appearance, but the Lord looks on the heart."

—1 Samuel 16:7

I will remember the works of the Lord; surely I will remember Your wonders of old.... Your way is through the sea, and Your path in the great waters, and your footsteps are not seen.

—Psalm 77:11, 19

Therefore, the Lord longs to be gracious to you, and therefore, He waits on high to have mercy on you; for the Lord is a God of justice; how blessed are all who long for Him.

—Isaiah 30:18

For I know the plans that I have for you, says the Lord, plans for peace and not for evil, to give you a future and a hope.

—Jeremiah 29:11

If you then, being evil, know how to give good gifts to your children, how much more will your Father who is in heaven give good things to those who ask Him!

—Matthew 7:11

PORNOGRAPHY

Turn away my eyes from beholding worthlessness, and revive me in Your way.

—Psalm 119:37

But I say to you that whoever looks on a woman to lust after her has committed adultery with her already in his heart.

—Matthew 5:28

Now the works of the flesh are revealed, which are these: adultery, sexual immorality, impurity, lewdness.

—Galatians 5:19

And do not have fellowship with the unfruitful works of darkness; instead, expose them. For it is shameful even to speak of those things which are done by them in secret.

—Ephesians 5:11–12

Marriage is to be honored among everyone, and the bed undefiled. But God will judge the sexually immoral and adulterers.

—Hebrews 13:4

POVERTY

Indeed, may he deliver the needy when he cries; the poor also, and him who has no helper. May he have compassion on the poor and needy, and save the lives of the needy.

—Psalm 72:12–13

He will regard the prayer of the destitute and will not despise their prayer.

—Psalm 102:17

Yet He raises up the poor from affliction and cares for their families like flocks of sheep.

—Psalm 107:41

He raises up the poor out of the dust and lifts the needy out of the ash heap.

—Psalm 113:7

I will abundantly bless her provisions; I will satisfy her poor with bread.

—Psalm 132:15

Sing to the Lord, praise the Lord. For He has delivered the soul of the poor from the hand of evildoers.

—Jeremiah 20:13

POWER

But, indeed, for this cause I have raised you up, in order to show in you My power and so that My name may be declared throughout all the earth.

—Exodus 9:16

Otherwise, you may say in your heart, "My power and the might of my hand have gained me this wealth." But you must remember the Lord your God, for it is He who gives you the

141

ability to get wealth, so that He may establish His covenant which He swore to your fathers, as it is today.

—Deuteronomy 8:17–18

To You, O Lord, is the greatness, and the power, and the glory, and the victory, and the majesty, for everything in the heavens and the earth is Yours. Yours is the kingdom, O Lord, and You exalt Yourself as head above all.

—1 Chronicles 29:11

He is wise in heart and mighty in strength. Who has hardened himself against Him and prospered?

—Job 9:4

O God, You are awesome from Your sanctuaries; the God of Israel is He who gives strength and power to people. Blessed be God!

—Psalm 68:35

POWER OF GOD'S WORD

My son, attend to my words; incline your ear to my sayings. Do not let them depart from your eyes; keep them in the midst of your heart; for they are life to those who find them, and health to all their body.

—Proverbs 4:20–22

Every word of God is pure; He is a shield to those who put their trust in Him.

—Proverbs 30:5

Heaven and earth will pass away, but My words will never pass away.

—Matthew 24:35

By the power of signs and wonders, by the power of the Spirit of God, so that from Jerusalem and as far around as Illyricum, I have fully preached the gospel of Christ.

—Romans 15:19

My speech and my preaching was not with enticing words of man's wisdom, but in demonstration of the Spirit and of power.

—1 Corinthians 2:4

For the word of God is alive, and active, and sharper than any two-edged sword, piercing even to the division of soul and spirit, of joints and marrow, and able to judge the thoughts and intents of the heart.

—Hebrews 4:12

POWER OF JESUS' NAME

Then Jesus came and spoke to them, saying, "All authority has been given to Me in heaven and on earth."

—Matthew 28:18

Truly, truly I say to you, he who believes in Me will do the works that I do also. And he will do greater works than these, because I am going to My Father. I will do whatever you ask in

My name, that the Father may be glorified in the Son. If you ask anything in My name, I will do it.

—John 14:12–14

On that day you will ask Me nothing. Truly, truly I say to you, whatever you ask the Father in My name, He will give it to you.

—John 16:23

Then Peter said, "I have no silver and gold, but I give you what I have. In the name of Jesus Christ of Nazareth, rise up and walk."

—Acts 3:6

Now, Lord, look on their threats and grant that Your servants may speak Your word with great boldness, by stretching out Your hand to heal and that signs and wonders may be performed in the name of Your holy Son Jesus.

—Acts 4:29–30

POWER OF PRAISE

You alone are the Lord. You have made heaven, the heaven of heavens, with all their host, the earth and all that is on it, the seas and all that are in them; and You preserve them all. And the host of heaven worships You.

—Nehemiah 9:6

Shout joyfully to God, all you lands! Sing out the glory of His name; make His praise glorious. Say to God, "How awesome are Your works! Through the greatness of Your power Your enemies cringe before You. All the earth will worship You and will sing to You; they will sing to Your name." Selah

—Psalm 66:1–4

I will greatly praise the Lord with my mouth; indeed, I will praise Him among the multitude. For He stands at the right hand of the poor, to save him from those who condemn his soul to death.

—Psalm 109:30–31

Praise the Lord! Praise God in His sanctuary; praise Him in the firmament of His power! Praise Him for His mighty acts; praise Him according to His excellent greatness! Praise Him with the sound of the trumpet; praise Him with the lyre and harp! Praise Him with the tambourine and dancing; praise Him with stringed instruments and flute! Praise Him with loud cymbals; praise Him with the clanging cymbals! Let everything that has breath praise the Lord. Praise the Lord!

—Psalm 150:1–6

Through Him, then, let us continually offer to God the sacrifice of praise, which is the fruit of our lips, giving thanks to His name.

—Hebrews 13:15

POWER OF THE TONGUE

A soft answer turns away wrath, but grievous words stir up anger.

—Proverbs 15:1

Death and life are in the power of the tongue, and those who love it will eat its fruit.

—Proverbs 18:21

Let no unwholesome word proceed out of your mouth, but only that which is good for building up, that it may give grace to the listeners.

—Ephesians 4:29

If anyone among you seems to be religious and does not bridle his tongue, but deceives his own heart, this man's religion is vain.

—James 1:26

For "He who wants to love life, and to see good days, let him keep his tongue from evil, and his lips from speaking deceit."

—1 Peter 3:10

PRAYER

From the depths I call on You, O Lord! O Lord, hear my voice; let Your ears be attentive to the sound of my supplications.

—Psalm 130:1–2

The LORD is near to all those who call upon Him, to all who call upon Him in truth. He will fulfill the desire of those who fear Him; He also will hear their cry and will save them.

—PSALM 145:18–19

But you, when you pray, enter your closet, and when you have shut your door, pray to your Father who is in secret. And your Father who sees in secret will reward you openly.

—MATTHEW 6:6

In the morning, rising up a great while before sunrise, He went out and departed to a solitary place. And there He prayed.

—MARK 1:35

On that day you will ask Me nothing. Truly, truly I say to you, whatever you ask the Father in My name, He will give it to you. Until now you have asked nothing in My name. Ask, and you will receive, that your joy may be full.

—JOHN 16:23–24

PRAYING FOR THE NATION

And on that day, says the LORD of Hosts, I will cut off the names of the idols from the land, and they will not be remembered any more. And I will also remove from the land the prophets and the unclean spirit.

—ZECHARIAH 13:2

He said to them, "You are those who justify yourselves before men, but God knows your hearts. For that which is highly esteemed before men is an abomination before God."

—Luke 16:15

"In the last days it shall be," says God, "that I will pour out My Spirit on all flesh; your sons and your daughters shall prophesy, your young men shall see visions, and your old men shall dream dreams. Even on My menservants and maidservants I will pour out My Spirit in those days; and they shall prophesy."

—Acts 2:17–18

Therefore I exhort first of all that you make supplications, prayers, intercessions, and thanksgivings for everyone, for kings and for all who are in authority, that we may lead a quiet and peaceful life in all godliness and honesty.

—1 Timothy 2:1–2

For I will be merciful toward their unrighteousness, and their sins and their lawless deeds I will remember no more.

—Hebrews 8:12

PRIDE

I tell you, this man went down to his house justified rather than the other. For everyone who exalts himself will be humbled, and he who humbles himself will be exalted.

—Luke 18:14

How can you believe, who receive glory from one another and do not seek the glory that comes from the only God?

—John 5:44

For I say, through the grace given to me, to everyone among you, not to think of himself more highly than he ought to think, but to think with sound judgment, according to the measure of faith God has distributed to every man.

—Romans 12:3

But, "Let him who boasts, boast in the Lord." For it is not he who commends himself who is approved, but he whom the Lord commends.

—2 Corinthians 10:17–18

But He gives more grace. For this reason it says, "God resists the proud, but gives grace to the humble."

—James 4:6

PRIORITIES

He who follows after righteousness and mercy finds life, righteousness, and honor.

—Proverbs 21:21

Prepare your work outside, and make it fit for yourself in the field; and afterwards build your house.

—Proverbs 24:27

For what does it profit a man if he gains the whole world and loses his own soul? Or what will a man give in exchange for his soul?

—Mark 8:36–37

Then He said to His disciples, "Therefore I say to you, do not be anxious for your life, what you will eat, nor for your body, what you will wear. Life is more than food, and the body is more than clothes. Consider the ravens: They neither sow nor reap, they have neither storehouses nor barns. Yet God feeds them. How much more valuable are you than birds?"

—Luke 12:22–24

For where your treasure is, there will your heart be also.

—Luke 12:34

PROSPEROUS

But you must remember the Lord your God, for it is He who gives you the ability to get wealth, so that He may establish His covenant which He swore to your fathers, as it is today.

—Deuteronomy 8:18

For you shall eat the fruit of the labor of your hands; you will be happy, and it shall be well with you.

—Psalm 128:2

The blessing of the Lord makes rich, and He adds no sorrow with it.

—Proverbs 10:22

He who is of a proud heart stirs up strife, but he who puts his trust in the LORD will prosper.

—PROVERBS 28:25

Bring all the tithes into the storehouse, that there may be food in My house, and test Me now in this, says the LORD of Hosts, if I will not open for you the windows of heaven and pour out for you a blessing, that there will not be room enough to receive it.

—MALACHI 3:10

PROTECTION

The LORD is my light and my salvation; whom will I fear? The LORD is the strength of my life; of whom will I be afraid?

—PSALM 27:1

The angel of the LORD camps around those who fear Him, and delivers them.

—PSALM 34:7

Because you have made the LORD, who is my refuge, even the Most High, your dwelling, there shall be no evil befall you, neither shall any plague come near your tent.

—PSALM 91:9–10

But whoever listens to me will dwell safely, and will be secure from fear of evil.

—PROVERBS 1:33

The name of the Lord is a strong tower; the righteous run into it and are safe.

—Proverbs 18:10

PROVISION

Now it will be, if you will diligently obey the voice of the Lord your God, being careful to do all His commandments which I am commanding you today, then the Lord your God will set you high above all the nations of the earth. And all these blessings will come on you and overtake you if you listen to the voice of the Lord your God.

—Deuteronomy 28:1–2

I have been young, and now am old; yet I have not seen the righteous forsaken, nor their offspring begging bread. The righteous are gracious and lend, and their offspring are a source of blessing.

—Psalm 37:25–26

God is able to make all grace abound toward you, so that you, always having enough of everything, may abound to every good work.

—2 Corinthians 9:8

I do not speak because I have need, for I have learned in whatever state I am to be content. I know both how to face humble circumstances and how to have abundance. Everywhere and in all things I have learned the secret, both to be full and to be hungry, both to abound and to suffer need.

—Philippians 4:11–12

But my God shall supply your every need according to His riches in glory by Christ Jesus.

—Philippians 4:19

PUNISHMENT

My son, do not despise the chastening of the Lord, nor be weary of His correction; for whom the Lord loves He corrects, even as a father the son in whom he delights.

—Proverbs 3:11–12

Your own wickedness will correct you, and your backslidings will reprove you. Know therefore and see that it is an evil thing and bitter for you to have forsaken the Lord your God, and the fear of Me is not in you, says the Lord God of Hosts.

—Jeremiah 2:19

But he who does wrong will receive for the wrong which he has done, and there is no partiality.

—Colossians 3:25

And to give you who are troubled rest with us when the Lord Jesus is revealed from heaven with His mighty angels, in flaming fire taking vengeance on those who do not know God and do not obey the gospel of our Lord Jesus Christ.

—2 Thessalonians 1:7–8

For if the word spoken by angels was true, and every sin and disobedience received a just recompense, how shall we escape if we neglect such a great salvation, which was first declared by the Lord, and was confirmed to us by those who heard Him?

—Hebrews 2:2–3

PURPOSE

The Lord will fulfill His purpose for me; Your mercy, O Lord, endures forever; do not forsake the works of Your hands.

—Psalm 138:8

The Lord has made all things for Himself, yes, even the wicked for the day of evil.

—Proverbs 16:4

For I know the plans that I have for you, says the Lord, plans for peace and not for evil, to give you a future and a hope.

—Jeremiah 29:11

We know that all things work together for good to those who love God, to those who are called according to His purpose.

—Romans 8:28

Just as He chose us in Him before the foundation of the world, to be holy and blameless before Him in love; He predestined us

154

to adoption as sons to Himself through Jesus Christ according to the good pleasure of His will.

—Ephesians 1:4–5

For we are His workmanship, created in Christ Jesus for good works, which God prepared beforehand, so that we should walk in them.

—Ephesians 2:10

RECONCILIATION

Now if your brother sins against you, go and tell him his fault between you and him alone. If he listens to you, you have gained your brother. But if he does not listen, then take with you one or two others, that by the testimony of two or three witnesses every word may be established. If he refuses to listen to them, tell it to the church. But if he refuses to listen even to the church, let him be to you as a Gentile and a tax collector.

—Matthew 18:15–17

For if while we were enemies, we were reconciled to God by the death of His Son, how much more, being reconciled, shall we be saved by His life.

—Romans 5:10

All this is from God, who has reconciled us to Himself through Jesus Christ and has given to us the ministry of reconciliation.

—2 Corinthians 5:18

And be kind one to another, tenderhearted, forgiving one another, just as God in Christ also forgave you.

—Ephesians 4:32

Pursue peace with all men, and the holiness without which no one will see the Lord.

—Hebrews 12:14

REDEMPTION

This is a faithful saying and worthy of all acceptance, that Christ Jesus came into the world to save sinners, of whom I am the worst.

—1 Timothy 1:15

So Christ was offered once to bear the sins of many, and He will appear a second time, not to bear sin but to save those who eagerly wait for Him.

—Hebrews 9:28

He Himself bore our sins in His own body on the tree, that we, being dead to sins, should live unto righteousness. "By His wounds you were healed."

—1 Peter 2:24

My little children, I am writing these things to you, so that you do not sin. But if anyone does sin, we have an Advocate with the Father, Jesus Christ the Righteous One. He is the atoning sacrifice for our sins, and not for ours only, but also for the sins of the whole world.

—1 John 2:1–2

You know that He was revealed to take away our sins, and in Him there is no sin.

—1 John 3:5

REJECTION

The righteous cry out, and the Lord hears, and delivers them out of all their troubles. The Lord is near to the broken-hearted, and saves the contrite of spirit. Many are the afflictions of the righteous, but the Lord delivers him out of them all. A righteous one keeps all his bones; not one of them is broken.

—Psalm 34:17–20

For the Lord will not forsake His people; neither will He abandon His inheritance.

—Psalm 94:14

If the world hates you, you know that it hated Me before it hated you.

—John 15:18

But He said to me, "My grace is sufficient for you, for My strength is made perfect in weakness." Therefore most gladly

I will boast in my weaknesses, that the power of Christ may rest upon me.

—2 Corinthians 12:9

Cast all your care upon Him, because He cares for you.

—1 Peter 5:7

RENOUNCING SEXUAL SIN

I urge you therefore, brothers, by the mercies of God, that you present your bodies as a living sacrifice, holy, and acceptable to God, which is your reasonable service of worship. Do not be conformed to this world, but be transformed by the renewing of your mind, that you may prove what is the good and acceptable and perfect will of God.

—Romans 12:1–2

Escape from sexual immorality. Every sin that a man commits is outside the body. But he who commits sexual immorality sins against his own body.

—1 Corinthians 6:18

I say then, walk in the Spirit, and you shall not fulfill the lust of the flesh.

—Galatians 5:16

Therefore put to death the parts of your earthly nature: sexual immorality, uncleanness, inordinate affection, evil desire, and covetousness, which is idolatry.

—Colossians 3:5

For this is the will of God, your sanctification: that you should abstain from sexual immorality…For God has not called us to uncleanness, but to holiness.

—1 Thessalonians 4:3, 7

REPENTANCE

If My people, who are called by My name, will humble themselves and pray, and seek My face and turn from their wicked ways, then I will hear from heaven, and will forgive their sin and will heal their land.

—2 Chronicles 7:14

I tell you, no! But unless you repent, you will all likewise perish.

—Luke 13:3

Peter said to them, "Repent and be baptized, every one of you, in the name of Jesus Christ for the forgiveness of sins, and you shall receive the gift of the Holy Spirit."

—Acts 2:38

Therefore repent and be converted, that your sins may be wiped away, that times of refreshing may come from the presence of the Lord.

—Acts 3:19

God overlooked the times of ignorance, but now He commands all men everywhere to repent.

—Acts 17:30

RESPECT

Honor your father and your mother, that your days may be long in the land which the Lord your God is giving you.

—Exodus 20:12

Therefore, everything you would like men to do to you, do also to them, for this is the Law and the Prophets.

—Matthew 7:12

All men should honor the Son, just as they honor the Father. He who does not honor the Son does not honor the Father who sent Him.

—John 5:23

Be devoted to one another with brotherly love; prefer one another in honor.

—Romans 12:10

Honor all people. Love the brotherhood. Fear God. Honor the king.

—1 Peter 2:17

Likewise, you husbands, live considerately with your wives, giving honor to the woman as the weaker vessel, since they too are also heirs of the grace of life, so that your prayers will not be hindered.

—1 Peter 3:7

REST

Remember the Sabbath day and keep it holy. Six days you shall labor and do all your work, but the seventh day is a Sabbath to the Lord your God. On it you shall not do any work, you, or your son, or your daughter, or your male servant, or your female servant, or your livestock, or your sojourner who is within your gates. For in six days the Lord made heaven and earth, the sea, and all that is in them, and rested on the seventh day. Therefore the Lord blessed the Sabbath day and made it holy.

—Exodus 20:8–11

It is in vain for you to rise up early, to stay up late, and to eat the bread of hard toil, for He gives sleep to His beloved.

—Psalm 127:2

Come to Me, all you who labor and are heavily burdened, and I will give you rest. Take My yoke upon you, and learn from Me. For I am meek and lowly in heart, and you will find rest for your souls. For My yoke is easy, and My burden is light.

—Matthew 11:28–30

Then He said to them, "Come away by yourselves to a remote place and rest a while," for many were coming and going, and they had no leisure even to eat.

—Mark 6:31

Therefore a rest remains for the people of God. For whoever enters His rest will also cease from his own works, as God did from His. Let us labor therefore to enter that rest, lest anyone fall by the same pattern of unbelief.

—Hebrews 4:9–11

RESTITUTION

If the sun has risen on him, then there is blood guilt for him. He must make full restitution. If he has nothing, then he will be sold for his theft. If the stolen item is in fact found alive in his possession, whether it be an ox, or donkey, or sheep, then he shall repay double.

—Exodus 22:3–4

Men do not despise a thief if he steals to satisfy himself when he is hungry. But if he is found, he will restore sevenfold; he will give all the substance of his house.

—Proverbs 6:30–31

Whoever, therefore, breaks one of the least of these commandments and teaches others to do likewise shall be called the least in the kingdom of heaven. But whoever does and teaches them shall be called great in the kingdom of heaven.

—Matthew 5:19

But Zacchaeus stood and said to the Lord, "Look, Lord, I give half of my possessions to the poor. And if I have taken anything from anyone by false accusation, I will repay him four times as much." Jesus said to him, "Today salvation has come to this house, because he also is a son of Abraham."

—Luke 19:8–9

Beloved, do not avenge yourselves, but rather give place to God's wrath, for it is written: "Vengeance is Mine. I will repay," says the Lord.

—Romans 12:19

REVENGE

You shall not take vengeance, nor bear any grudge against the children of your people, but you shall love your neighbor as yourself: I am the Lord.

—Leviticus 19:18

Vengeance is Mine, and recompense. Their foot will slip in due time; for the day of their calamity is at hand, and the things to come hasten upon them.

—Deuteronomy 32:35

Do not rejoice when your enemy falls, and do not let your heart be glad when he stumbles.

—Proverbs 24:17

You have heard that it was said, "An eye for an eye, and a tooth for a tooth." But I say to you, do not resist an evil person. But whoever strikes you on your right cheek, turn to him the other as well. And if anyone sues you in a court of law and takes

163

away your tunic, let him have your cloak also. And whoever compels you to go a mile, go with him two.

—Matthew 5:38–41

Beloved, do not avenge yourselves, but rather give place to God's wrath, for it is written: "Vengeance is Mine. I will repay," says the Lord.

—Romans 12:19

RIGHTEOUS LIVING

Only carefully obey the commandment and the law that Moses the servant of the Lord commanded you: to love the Lord your God, to walk in all His ways, to obey His commandments, to cling to Him, and to serve Him with all your heart and soul.

—Joshua 22:5

Blessed is the man who walks not in the counsel of the ungodly, nor stands in the path of sinners, nor sits in the seat of scoffers; but his delight is in the law of the Lord, and in His law he meditates day and night.

—Psalm 1:1–2

For the Lord God is a sun and shield; the Lord will give favor and glory, for no good thing will He withhold from the one who walks uprightly.

—Psalm 84:11

He who trusts in his riches will fall, but the righteous will flourish as a branch.

—Proverbs 11:28

And this I pray, that your love may abound yet more and more in knowledge and in all discernment, that you may approve things that are excellent so that you may be pure and blameless for the day of Christ.

—Philippians 1:9–10

ROLE MODELS

My son, keep my words, and lay up my commandments within you. Keep my commandments and live, and my teaching as the apple of your eye. Bind them on your fingers, write them on the tablet of your heart.

—Proverbs 7:1–3

But it shall not be so among you. Whoever would be great among you must be your servant, and whoever among you would be greatest must be servant of all.

—Mark 10:43–44

For I would that all men were even as I myself. But every man has his proper gift from God, one after this manner and another after that.

—1 Corinthians 7:7

Therefore be imitators of God as beloved children. Walk in love, as Christ loved us and gave Himself for us as a fragrant offering and a sacrifice to God.

—Ephesians 5:1–2

In all things presenting yourself as an example of good works: in doctrine showing integrity, gravity, incorruptibility, and sound speech that cannot be condemned, so that the one who opposes you may be ashamed, having nothing evil to say of you.

—Titus 2:7–8

SATISFACTION

Bless the Lord, O my soul, and all that is within me, bless His holy name. Bless the Lord, O my soul, and forget not all His benefits, who forgives all your iniquities, who heals all your diseases, who redeems your life from the pit, who crowns you with lovingkindness and tender mercies, who satisfies your mouth with good things, so that your youth is renewed like the eagle's.

—Psalm 103:1–5

And the Lord shall guide you continually, and satisfy your soul in drought, and strengthen your bones; and you shall be like a watered garden, and like a spring of water, whose waters do not fail.

—Isaiah 58:11

Blessed are those who hunger and thirst for righteousness, for they shall be filled.

—Matthew 5:6

Jesus said to them, "I am the bread of life. Whoever comes to Me shall never hunger, and whoever believes in Me shall never thirst."

—John 6:35

Now faith is the substance of things hoped for, the evidence of things not seen.

—Hebrews 11:1

But if we walk in the light as He is in the light, we have fellowship one with another, and the blood of Jesus Christ His Son cleanses us from all sin.

—1 John 1:7

SEEKING GOD

But if from there you will seek the Lord your God, you will find Him, if you seek Him with all your heart and with all your soul.

—Deuteronomy 4:29

As for you, Solomon my son, know the God of your fathers and serve Him with a whole heart and with a willing spirit, for the Lord searches every heart and understands the intent of every thought. If you seek Him, He will be found by you, but if you forsake Him, He will abandon you forever.

—1 Chronicles 28:9

Those who know Your name will put their trust in You, for You, Lord, have not forsaken those who seek You.

—Psalm 9:10

I love those who love me, and those who seek me early will find me.

—Proverbs 8:17

You shall seek Me and find Me, when you shall search for Me with all your heart. I will be found by you, says the Lord, and I will turn away your captivity and gather you from all the nations and from all the places where I have driven you, says the Lord, and I will bring you back into the place from where I caused you to be carried away captive.

—Jeremiah 29:13–14

SELF-CONTROL

Judge me, O Lord, for I have walked in my integrity. I have trusted in the Lord; I will not slip. Examine me, O Lord, and test me; try my affections and my heart.

—Psalm 26:1–2

A fool utters all his mind, but a wise man keeps it in until afterwards.

—Proverbs 29:11

But I bring and keep my body under subjection, lest when preaching to others I myself should be disqualified.

—1 Corinthians 9:27

But the fruit of the Spirit is love, joy, peace, patience, gentleness, goodness, faith, meekness, and self-control; against such there is no law.

—Galatians 5:22–23

For this reason make every effort to add virtue to your faith; and to your virtue, knowledge; and to your knowledge, self-control; and to your self-control, patient endurance; and to your patient endurance, godliness; and to your godliness, brotherly kindness; and to your brotherly kindness, love. For if these things reside in you and abound, they ensure that you will neither be useless nor unfruitful in the knowledge of our Lord Jesus Christ.

—2 Peter 1:5–8

SELF-DENIAL

Then Jesus said to His disciples, "If anyone will come after Me, let him deny himself, and take up his cross, and follow Me. For whoever would save his life will lose it, and whoever loses his life for My sake will find it. For what will it profit a man if he gains the whole world and loses his own soul? Or what shall a man give in exchange for his soul?"

—Matthew 16:24–26

He said to them, "Truly, I tell you, there is no man who has left his home or parents or brothers or wife or children, for the sake of the kingdom of God, who shall not receive many times more in this age and, in the age to come, eternal life."

—Luke 18:29–30

Therefore, brothers, we are debtors not to the flesh, to live according to the flesh. For if you live according to the flesh, you will die, but if through the Spirit you put to death the deeds of the body, you will live.

—Romans 8:12–13

Those who are Christ's have crucified the flesh with its passions and lusts.

—Galatians 5:24

For the grace of God that brings salvation has appeared to all men, teaching us that, denying ungodliness and worldly desires, we should live soberly, righteously, and in godliness in this present world.

—Titus 2:11–12

SELF-IMAGE

I will praise you, for You made me with fear and wonder; marvelous are Your works, and You know me completely. My frame was not hidden from You when I was made in secret, and intricately put together in the lowest parts of the earth.

Your eyes saw me unformed, yet in Your book all my days were written, before any of them came into being.

—Psalm 139:14–16

For as he thinks in his heart, so is he. "Eat and drink!" he says to you, but his heart is not with you.

—Proverbs 23:7

I am the vine, you are the branches. He who remains in Me, and I in him, bears much fruit. For without Me you can do nothing.

—John 15:5

For those whom He foreknew, He predestined to be conformed to the image of His Son, so that He might be the firstborn among many brothers.

—Romans 8:29

For we are His workmanship, created in Christ Jesus for good works, which God prepared beforehand, so that we should walk in them.

—Ephesians 2:10

SELF-RIGHTEOUSNESS

The way of a fool is right in his own eyes, but he who listens to counsel is wise.

—Proverbs 12:15

Do you see a man wise in his own conceit? There is more hope for a fool than for him.

—Proverbs 26:12

Let another man praise you, and not your own mouth; a stranger, and not your own lips.

—Proverbs 27:2

But, "Let him who boasts, boast in the Lord." For it is not he who commends himself who is approved, but he whom the Lord commends.

—2 Corinthians 10:17–18

For if someone thinks himself to be something when he is nothing, he deceives himself.

—Galatians 6:3

SELF-WORTH

Then God said, "Let us make man in our image, after our likeness, and let them have dominion over the fish of the sea, and over the birds of the air, and over the livestock, and over all the earth, and over every creeping thing that creeps on the earth." So God created man in His own image; in the image of God He created him; male and female He created them.

—Genesis 1:26–27

What is man that You are mindful of him, and the son of man that You attend to him? For You have made him a little lower than the angels, and crowned him with glory and honor. You grant him dominion over the works of Your hands; You have put all things under his feet.

—Psalm 8:4–6

You brought my inner parts into being; You wove me in my mother's womb. I will praise you, for You made me with fear and wonder; marvelous are Your works, and You know me completely.

—Psalm 139:13–14

Are not two sparrows sold for a penny? And not one of them will fall to the ground without your Father. But the very hairs of your head are all numbered. Therefore do not fear. You are more valuable than many sparrows.

—Matthew 10:29–31

For we are His workmanship, created in Christ Jesus for good works, which God prepared beforehand, so that we should walk in them.

—Ephesians 2:10

SERVANTHOOD

You must follow after the Lord your God, fear Him, and keep His commandments, obey His voice, and you must serve Him, and cling to Him.

—Deuteronomy 13:4

Only carefully obey the commandment and the law that Moses the servant of the Lord commanded you: to love the

Lord your God, to walk in all His ways, to obey His commandments, to cling to Him, and to serve Him with all your heart and soul.

—Joshua 22:5

It shall not be so among you. Whoever would be great among you, let him serve you, and whoever would be first among you, let him be your slave, even as the Son of Man did not come to be served, but to serve and to give His life as a ransom for many.

—Matthew 20:26–28

But it shall not be so among you. Whoever would be great among you must be your servant, and whoever among you would be greatest must be servant of all.

—Mark 10:43–44

For I have given you an example, that you should do as I have done to you. Truly, truly I say to you, a servant is not greater than his master, nor is he who is sent greater than he who sent him.

—John 13:15–16

SEXUAL INTIMACY

Therefore a man will leave his father and his mother and be joined to his wife, and they will become one flesh.

—Genesis 2:24

What? Do you not know that your body is the temple of the Holy Spirit, who is in you, whom you have received from God, and that you are not your own? You were bought with a price. Therefore glorify God in your body and in your spirit, which are God's.

—1 CORINTHIANS 6:19–20

The wife does not have authority over her own body, but the husband does. Likewise, the husband does not have authority over his own body, but the wife does. Do not deprive one another except with consent for a time, that you may give yourselves to fasting and prayer. Then come together again, so that Satan does not tempt you for lack of self-control.

—1 CORINTHIANS 7:4–5

In this way men ought to love their wives as their own bodies. He who loves his wife loves himself. For no one ever hated his own flesh, but nourishes and cherishes it, just as the Lord cares for the church.

—EPHESIANS 5:28–29

Marriage is to be honored among everyone, and the bed undefiled. But God will judge the sexually immoral and adulterers.

—HEBREWS 13:4

SHAME

At the evening sacrifice I rose up from my heaviness and, despite having my clothes and my robe torn, I knelt on my knees and stretched out my hands in prayer to the Lord my God and said: "O my God, I am ashamed and embarrassed to lift up my face to You, my God, because our iniquities have expanded over our heads and our wrongdoing has grown up to the heavens."

—Ezra 9:5–6

Then I shall not be ashamed, when I have my focus on all Your commandments.

—Psalm 119:6

Let my heart be blameless in Your statutes, that I may not be ashamed.

—Psalm 119:80

Do not fear, for you shall not be ashamed nor be humiliated; for you shall not be put to shame, for you shall forget the shame of your youth and shall not remember the reproach of your widowhood anymore. For your Maker is your husband. The Lord of Hosts is His name; and your Redeemer is the Holy One of Israel; He shall be called the God of the whole earth.

—Isaiah 54:4–5

For the Scripture says, "Whoever believes in Him will not be ashamed."

—Romans 10:11

SLANDER

He will bring forth your righteousness as the light, and your judgment as the noonday.

—Psalm 37:6

Listen to Me, you who know righteousness, the people in whose heart is My law; do not fear the reproach of men nor be afraid of their revilings.

—Isaiah 51:7

Blessed are you when men revile you, and persecute you, and say all kinds of evil against you falsely for My sake. Rejoice and be very glad, because great is your reward in heaven, for in this manner they persecuted the prophets who were before you.

—Matthew 5:11–12

You will be hated by all men for My name's sake. But he who endures to the end will be saved.

—Matthew 10:22

If you are reproached because of the name of Christ, you are blessed, because the Spirit of glory and of God rests upon you. On their part He is blasphemed, but on your part He is glorified.

—1 Peter 4:14

SPEECH

Who is the man who desires life, and loves a long life in order to see good? Keep your tongue from evil, and your lips from speaking deceit. Turn away from evil, and do good; seek peace, and pursue it.

—Psalm 34:12–14

Let no unwholesome word proceed out of your mouth, but only that which is good for building up, that it may give grace to the listeners.

—Ephesians 4:29

Do all things without murmuring and disputing.

—Philippians 2:14

Let your speech always be with grace, seasoned with salt, that you may know how you should answer everyone.

—Colossians 4:6

We all err in many ways. But if any man does not err in word, he is a perfect man and able also to control the whole body. See how we put bits in the mouths of horses that they may obey us, and we control their whole bodies.

—James 3:2–3

SPIRITUAL GROWTH

Blessed is the man who walks not in the counsel of the ungodly, nor stands in the path of sinners, nor sits in the seat of scoffers;

but his delight is in the law of the Lord, and in His law he meditates day and night. He will be like a tree planted by the rivers of water, that brings forth its fruit in its season; its leaf will not wither, and whatever he does will prosper.

—Psalm 1:1–3

But whoever drinks of the water that I shall give him will never thirst. Indeed, the water that I shall give him will become in him a well of water springing up into eternal life.

—John 4:14

But, speaking the truth in love, we may grow up in all things into Him, who is the head, Christ Himself, from whom the whole body is joined together and connected by every joint and ligament, as every part effectively does its work and grows, building itself up in love.

—Ephesians 4:15–16

For this reason we also, since the day we heard it, do not cease to pray for you and to ask that you may be filled with the knowledge of His will in all wisdom and spiritual understanding; that you may walk in a manner worthy of the Lord, pleasing to all, being fruitful in every good work, and increasing in the knowledge of God.

—Colossians 1:9–10

But grow in the grace and knowledge of our Lord and Savior Jesus Christ. To Him be glory, both now and forever. Amen.

—2 Peter 3:18

STABILITY

He who walks uprightly walks surely, but he who perverts his ways will be known.

—Proverbs 10:9

The wicked flee when no man pursues, but the righteous are bold as a lion. Because of the transgression of a land, many are its princes; but by a man of understanding and knowledge, it shall be prolonged.

—Proverbs 28:1–2

Therefore we should be more attentive to what we have heard, lest we drift away.

—Hebrews 2:1

Therefore, since we are receiving a kingdom that cannot be moved, let us be gracious, by which we may serve God acceptably with reverence and godly fear.

—Hebrews 12:28

Whoever loves his brother lives in the light, and in him there is no cause for stumbling.

—1 John 2:10

STANDING AGAINST WORLDLINESS

If you were of the world, the world would love you as its own. But because you are not of the world, since I chose you out of the world, the world therefore hates you.

—John 15:19

Do not be conformed to this world, but be transformed by the renewing of your mind, that you may prove what is the good and acceptable and perfect will of God.

—Romans 12:2

Set your affection on things above, not on things on earth.

—Colossians 3:2

Teaching us that, denying ungodliness and worldly desires, we should live soberly, righteously, and in godliness in this present world.

—Titus 2:12

Do not love the world or the things in the world. If anyone loves the world, the love of the Father is not in him. For all that is in the world—the lust of the flesh, the lust of the eyes, and the pride of life—is not of the Father, but is of the world. The world and its desires are passing away, but the one who does the will of God lives forever.

—1 John 2:15–17

STRENGTH

Be strong and of a good courage. Fear not, nor be afraid of them, for the Lord your God, it is He who goes with you. He will not fail you, nor forsake you.

—Deuteronomy 31:6

Riches and honor flow from You, and You rule over all. In Your hand are power and might, and in Your hand it is to make great and to strengthen all.

—1 Chronicles 29:12

The righteous also will hold to his way, and he who has clean hands will be stronger and stronger.

—Job 17:9

But those who wait upon the Lord shall renew their strength; they shall mount up with wings as eagles, they shall run and not be weary, and they shall walk and not faint.

—Isaiah 40:31

Do not fear, for I am with you; do not be dismayed, for I am your God. I will strengthen you, I will help you, yes, I will uphold you with My righteous right hand.

—Isaiah 41:10

STRESS

Except the Lord build the house, those who build labor in vain; except the Lord guards the city, the watchman stays awake in vain. It is in vain for you to rise up early, to stay up late, and to eat the bread of hard toil, for He gives sleep to His beloved.

—Psalm 127:1–2

Do not fear, for I am with you; do not be dismayed, for I am your God. I will strengthen you, I will help you, yes, I will uphold you with My righteous right hand.

—Isaiah 41:10

Then He said to them, "Come away by yourselves to a remote place and rest a while," for many were coming and going, and they had no leisure even to eat.

—Mark 6:31

Peace I leave with you. My peace I give to you. Not as the world gives do I give to you. Let not your heart be troubled, neither let it be afraid.

—John 14:27

We know that all things work together for good to those who love God, to those who are called according to His purpose.

—Romans 8:28

SUCCESS

I am going the way of all the earth. Be strong, and show yourself to be a man. And keep the charge of the Lord your God, walking in His ways, keeping His statutes, His commandments, His judgments, and His testimonies, as it is written in the Law of Moses, that you may prosper in all that you do and wherever you turn.

—1 Kings 2:2–3

And in every deed that he undertook in the service of the house of God and with the law and commandment to seek out his God, he did this with all his heart, and he found success.

—2 Chronicles 31:21

For you shall eat the fruit of the labor of your hands; you will be happy, and it shall be well with you.

—Psalm 128:2

And also everyone to whom God has given wealth and possessions, and given him power to enjoy them, and to receive his reward and to rejoice in his labor—this is the gift of God.

—Ecclesiastes 5:19

They shall build houses and inhabit them; and they shall plant vineyards and eat the fruit of them. They shall not build and another inhabit; they shall not plant and another eat; for as the days of a tree are the days of My people, and My chosen ones shall long enjoy the work of their hands.

—Isaiah 65:21–22

TALENTS

For the LORD God is a sun and shield; the LORD will give favor and glory, for no good thing will He withhold from the one who walks uprightly.

—PSALM 84:11

A man's gift makes room for him, and brings him before great men.

—PROVERBS 18:16

For to a man who is pleasing before Him, God gives wisdom, knowledge, and joy; but to the sinner He gives the work of gathering and collecting to give him who is pleasing before God. Also this is vanity and chasing the wind.

—ECCLESIASTES 2:26

We have diverse gifts according to the grace that is given to us: if prophecy, according to the proportion of faith; if service, in serving; he who teaches, in teaching; he who exhorts, in exhortation; he who gives, with generosity; he who rules, with diligence; he who shows mercy, with cheerfulness.

—ROMANS 12:6–8

For I would that all men were even as I myself. But every man has his proper gift from God, one after this manner and another after that.

—1 CORINTHIANS 7:7

TEMPTATION

I have told you these things so that in Me you may have peace. In the world you will have tribulation. But be of good cheer. I have overcome the world.

—John 16:33

My brothers, count it all joy when you fall into diverse temptations, knowing that the trying of your faith develops patience. But let patience perfect its work, that you may be perfect and complete, lacking nothing.

—James 1:2–4

Blessed is the man who endures temptation, for when he is tried, he will receive the crown of life, which the Lord has promised to those who love Him. Let no man say when he is tempted, "I am tempted by God," for God cannot be tempted with evil; neither does He tempt anyone. But each man is tempted when he is drawn away by his own lust and enticed. Then, when lust has conceived, it brings forth sin; and when sin is finished, it brings forth death.

—James 1:12–15

Then the Lord knows how to rescue the godly from trial, and to keep the unrighteous under punishment for the Day of Judgment.

—2 Peter 2:9

Because you have kept My word of patience, I also will keep you from the hour of temptation which shall come upon the entire world, to test those who dwell on the earth.

—Revelation 3:10

THANKFULNESS

You are to celebrate the festival for seven days to the Lord your God in the place where the Lord will choose, because the Lord your God will bless you in all your produce, and in all the works of your hands. Therefore, you will indeed rejoice.

—Deuteronomy 16:15

Give thanks to the Lord, call on His name; make known His deeds among the peoples.

—1 Chronicles 16:8

Enter into His gates with thanksgiving, and into His courts with praise; be thankful to Him, and bless His name.

—Psalm 100:4

Be anxious for nothing, but in everything, by prayer and supplication with gratitude, make your requests known to God.

—Philippians 4:6

Through Him, then, let us continually offer to God the sacrifice of praise, which is the fruit of our lips, giving thanks to His name.

—Hebrews 13:15

TIME

So teach us to number our days, that we may apply our hearts to wisdom.

—Psalm 90:12

To everything there is a season, a time for every purpose under heaven.

—Ecclesiastes 3:1

I must do the works of Him who sent Me while it is day. Night is coming when no one can work.

—John 9:4

Come now, you who say, "Today or tomorrow we will go into this city, spend a year there, buy and sell, and make a profit," whereas you do not know what will happen tomorrow. What is your life? It is just a vapor that appears for a little while and then vanishes away. Instead you ought to say, "If the Lord wills, we shall live and do this or that."

—James 4:13–15

But grow in the grace and knowledge of our Lord and Savior Jesus Christ. To Him be glory, both now and forever. Amen.

—2 Peter 3:18

TRIALS

Not only so, but we also boast in tribulation, knowing that tribulation produces patience, patience produces character, and character produces hope. And hope does not disappoint, because the love of God is shed abroad in our hearts by the Holy Spirit who has been given to us.

—Romans 5:3–5

No temptation has taken you except what is common to man. God is faithful, and He will not permit you to be tempted above what you can endure, but will with the temptation also make a way to escape, that you may be able to bear it.

—1 Corinthians 10:13

My brothers, count it all joy when you fall into diverse temptations, knowing that the trying of your faith develops patience. But let patience perfect its work, that you may be perfect and complete, lacking nothing.

—James 1:2–4

Blessed is the man who endures temptation, for when he is tried, he will receive the crown of life, which the Lord has promised to those who love Him.

—James 1:12

Beloved, do not be surprised at the fiery ordeal that is taking place among you to test you, as though some strange thing happened to you. But rejoice in so far as you share in Christ's sufferings, so that you may rejoice and be glad also in the revelation of His glory.

—1 Peter 4:12–13

TROUBLE

The Lord is my pillar, and my fortress, and my deliverer; my God, my rock, in whom I take refuge; my shield, and the horn of my salvation, my high tower. I will call on the Lord, who is worthy to be praised, and I will be saved from my enemies.

—Psalm 18:2–3

For in the time of trouble He will hide me in His pavilion; in the shelter of His tabernacle He will hide me; He will set me up on a rock.

—Psalm 27:5

I will be glad and rejoice in Your lovingkindness, for You have seen my trouble; You have known my soul in adversities....Be gracious to me, O Lord, for I am in trouble; my eye wastes away with grief, yes, my soul and my body.

—Psalm 31:7–9

But the salvation of the righteous is from the Lord; He is their refuge in the time of distress. The Lord will help them and deliver them; He will deliver them from the wicked, and save them, because they take refuge in Him.

—Psalm 37:39–40

God is our refuge and strength, a well-proven help in trouble.

—Psalm 46:1

TRUST

The God of my strength, in whom I will trust; my shield and the horn of my salvation, my fortress and my sanctuary; my Savior, You save me from violence.

—2 SAMUEL 22:3

Oh, taste and see that the LORD is good; blessed is the man who takes refuge in Him.

—PSALM 34:8

Blessed is the man who places trust in the LORD, but does not turn toward the proud, nor those falling away to falsehood.

—PSALM 40:4

Trust in the LORD with all your heart, and lean not on your own understanding; in all your ways acknowledge Him, and He will direct your paths.

—PROVERBS 3:5–6

Blessed is the man who trusts in the LORD, and whose hope is the LORD. For he shall be as a tree planted by the waters, and that spreads out its roots by the river, and shall not fear when heat comes, but its leaf shall be green, and it shall not be anxious in the year of drought, neither shall cease from yielding fruit.

—JEREMIAH 17:7–8

UNBELIEVING SPOUSE

Remove your way far from her, and do not go near the door of her house, lest you give your honor to others, and your years to the cruel; lest strangers be filled with your wealth, and your labors go to the house of a stranger;

—Proverbs 5:8–10

For the Lord, the God of Israel, says that He hates divorce; for it covers one's garment with violence, says the Lord of Hosts. Therefore take heed to your spirit, that you do not deal treacherously.

—Malachi 2:16

But I say to you, whoever divorces his wife, except for sexual immorality, and marries another, commits adultery. And whoever marries her who is divorced commits adultery.

—Matthew 19:9

He said to them, "Whoever divorces his wife and marries another commits adultery against her. And if a woman divorces her husband and marries another, she commits adultery."

—Mark 10:11–12

To the rest I speak, not the Lord: If any brother has an unbelieving wife who consents to live with him, he should not divorce her. And if the woman has an unbelieving husband who consents to live with her, she should not divorce him. For the unbelieving husband is sanctified by the wife, and the unbelieving wife is sanctified by the husband. Otherwise, your children would be unclean. But now they are holy.

—1 Corinthians 7:12–14

UNDERSTANDING

Discretion will preserve you; understanding will keep you, to deliver you from the way of the evil man, from the man who speaks perverse things, from those who leave the paths of uprightness to walk in the ways of darkness.

—Proverbs 2:11–13

He who is slow to wrath is of great understanding, but he who is hasty of spirit exalts folly.

—Proverbs 14:29

He who has knowledge spares his words, and a man of understanding is of an excellent spirit.

—Proverbs 17:27

A fool has no delight in understanding, but in expressing his own heart.

—Proverbs 18:2

Counsel in the heart of man is like deep water, but a man of understanding will draw it out.

—Proverbs 20:5

Let your speech always be with grace, seasoned with salt, that you may know how you should answer everyone.

—Colossians 4:6

UNPARDONABLE SIN

Truly I say to you, all sins will be forgiven the sons of men, and whatever blasphemies they speak.

—Mark 3:28

For it is impossible for those who were once enlightened, who have tasted the heavenly gift, who shared in the Holy Spirit, and have tasted the good word of God and the powers of the age to come, if they fall away, to be renewed once more to repentance, since they again crucify to themselves the Son of God and subject Him to public shame.

—Hebrews 6:4–6

How much more severe a punishment do you suppose he deserves, who has trampled under foot the Son of God, and has regarded the blood of the covenant that sanctified him to be a common thing, and has insulted the Spirit of grace?

—Hebrews 10:29

For if after they have escaped the defilements of the world through the knowledge of the Lord and Savior Jesus Christ, and they are again entangled in them and are overcome, the latter end is worse for them than the beginning.

—2 Peter 2:20

The Lord is not slow concerning His promise, as some count slowness. But He is patient with us, because He does not want any to perish, but all to come to repentance.

—2 Peter 3:9

VALUES

The Lord requites to every man his right conduct and loyalty. So the Lord gave you into my hand today, but I am not willing to stretch my hand against the Lord's anointed.

—1 Samuel 26:23

Blessed is the man who walks not in the counsel of the ungodly, nor stands in the path of sinners, nor sits in the seat of scoffers; but his delight is in the law of the Lord, and in His law he meditates day and night. He will be like a tree planted by the rivers of water, that brings forth its fruit in its season; its leaf will not wither, and whatever he does will prosper.

—Psalm 1:1–3

Better is the poor who walks in his uprightness, than he who is perverse in his ways, though he be rich.

—Proverbs 28:6

Thus says the Lord Stand in the ways and see, and ask for the old paths where the good way is and walk in it, and you shall find rest for your souls. But they said, "We will not walk in it."

—Jeremiah 6:16

He has told you, O man, what is good—and what does the Lord require of you, but to do justice and to love kindness, and to walk humbly with your God?

—Micah 6:8

VICTORY

For the Lord your God is He that goes with you, to fight for you against your enemies, to save you.

—Deuteronomy 20:4

Through God we shall be valiant, for He shall tread down our enemies.

—Psalm 108:13

No temptation has taken you except what is common to man. God is faithful, and He will not permit you to be tempted above what you can endure, but will with the temptation also make a way to escape, that you may be able to bear it.

—1 Corinthians 10:13

But He said to me, "My grace is sufficient for you, for My strength is made perfect in weakness." Therefore most gladly I will boast in my weaknesses, that the power of Christ may rest upon me. So I take pleasure in weaknesses, in reproaches, in hardships, in persecutions, and in distresses for Christ's sake. For when I am weak, then I am strong.

—2 Corinthians 12:9–10

I can do all things because of Christ who strengthens me.

—Philippians 4:13

WAITING ON THE PROMISE

Rest in the Lord, and wait patiently for Him; do not fret because of those who prosper in their way, because of those who make wicked schemes.

—Psalm 37:7

Now, Lord, what do I wait for? My hope is in You.

—Psalm 39:7

But those who wait upon the Lord shall renew their strength; they shall mount up with wings as eagles, they shall run and not be weary, and they shall walk and not faint.

—Isaiah 40:31

But as for me, I watch for the Lord; I await the God of my salvation; my God will hear me.

—Micah 7:7

For the vision is yet for an appointed time; but it speaks of the end, and does not lie. If it delays, wait for it; it will surely come, it will not delay.

—Habakkuk 2:3

WALKING IN GOD'S WAYS

The righteous shall flourish like the palm tree and grow like a cedar in Lebanon.

—Psalm 92:12

Many people shall go and say, "Come, and let us go up to the mountain of the Lord, to the house of the God of Jacob, and He will teach us of His ways, and we will walk in His paths." For out of Zion shall go forth the law, and the word of the Lord from Jerusalem.

—Isaiah 2:3

For you were formerly darkness, but now you are light in the Lord. Walk as children of light.

—Ephesians 5:8

See then that you walk carefully, not as fools, but as wise men.

—Ephesians 5:15

Walk in wisdom toward those who are outside, wisely using the opportunity.

—Colossians 4:5

So that you may walk honestly toward those who are outsiders and that you may lack nothing.

—1 Thessalonians 4:12

WAR

He shall judge among the nations, and shall rebuke many peoples; and they shall beat their swords into plowshares, and their spears into pruning hooks; nation shall not lift up sword against nation, nor shall they learn war any more.

—Isaiah 2:4

Blessed are the peacemakers, for they shall be called the sons of God.

—Matthew 5:9

Therefore I exhort first of all that you make supplications, prayers, intercessions, and thanksgivings for everyone, for kings and for all who are in authority, that we may lead a quiet and peaceful life in all godliness and honesty.

—1 Timothy 2:1–2

Where do wars and fights among you come from? Do they not come from your lusts that war in your body? You lust and do not have, so you kill. You desire to have and cannot obtain. You fight and war. Yet you do not have, because you do not ask. You ask, and do not receive, because you ask amiss, that you may spend it on your passions.

—James 4:1–3

Submit yourselves to every human authority for the Lord's sake, whether it be to the king, as supreme, or to governors, as sent by him for the punishment of evildoers and to praise those who do right.

—1 Peter 2:13–14

WEALTH

A good man leaves an inheritance to his children's children, and the wealth of the sinner is laid up for the just.

—Proverbs 13:22

The rich rules over the poor, and the borrower is servant to the lender.

—Proverbs 22:7

Do not store up for yourselves treasures on earth where moth and rust destroy and where thieves break in and steal. But store up for yourselves treasures in heaven, where neither moth nor rust destroy and where thieves do not break in nor steal, for where your treasure is, there will your heart be also.

—Matthew 6:19–21

No one can serve two masters. For either he will hate the one and love the other, or else he will hold to the one and despise the other. You cannot serve God and money.

—Matthew 6:24

For the love of money is the root of all evil. While coveting after money, some have strayed from the faith and pierced themselves through with many sorrows.

—1 Timothy 6:10

WIDOWERS

You shall not afflict any widow or orphan. If you afflict them in any way and they cry at all to Me, I will surely hear their cry. And My anger will burn, and I will kill you with the sword, and your wives will become widows, and your children fatherless.

—Exodus 22:22–24

A father of the fatherless, and a protector of the widows, is God in His holy habitation.

—Psalm 68:5

Learn to do good; seek justice, relieve the oppressed; judge the fatherless, plead for the widow.

—Isaiah 1:17

Do not oppress the widow, orphan, sojourner, or poor. And let none of you contemplate evil deeds in your hearts against his brother.

—Zechariah 7:10

Honor widows that are widows indeed. But if any widow has children or grandchildren, let them learn first to show piety at home and to repay their parents. For this is good and acceptable before God. Now she who is a widow indeed, and desolate, trusts in God, and continues in supplications and prayers night and day. But she who lives in pleasure is dead while she lives.

—1 Timothy 5:3–6

WILL OF GOD

I delight to do Your will, O my God; Your law is within my inward parts.

—Psalm 40:8

For the Lord God is a sun and shield; the Lord will give favor and glory, for no good thing will He withhold from the one who walks uprightly.

—Psalm 84:11

Your word is a lamp to my feet, and a light to my path.

—Psalm 119:105

Cause me to hear Your lovingkindness in the morning; for in You I have my trust; cause me to know the way I should walk, for I lift up my soul unto You.

—Psalm 143:8

"If you love Me, keep My commandments."…Jesus answered him, "If a man loves Me, he will keep My word. My Father will love him, and We will come to him, and make Our home with him."

—John 14:15, 23

In everything give thanks, for this is the will of God in Christ Jesus concerning you.

—1 Thessalonians 5:18

WISDOM

From where then does wisdom come? And where is the place of understanding? It is hidden from the eyes of all living and concealed from the birds of the air.

—Job 28:20–21

I will instruct you and teach you in the way which you should go; I will counsel you with my eye on you.

—Psalm 32:8

So shall the knowledge of wisdom be to your soul; when you have found it, then there will be a reward, and your expectation will not be cut off.

—Proverbs 24:14

For to a man who is pleasing before Him, God gives wisdom, knowledge, and joy; but to the sinner He gives the work of gathering and collecting to give him who is pleasing before God. Also this is vanity and chasing the wind.

—Ecclesiastes 2:26

If any of you lacks wisdom, let him ask of God, who gives to all men liberally and without criticism, and it will be given to him.

—James 1:5

WITNESSING

Go therefore and make disciples of all nations, baptizing them in the name of the Father and of the Son and of the Holy

Spirit, teaching them to observe all things I have commanded you. And remember, I am with you always, even to the end of the age. Amen.

—Matthew 28:19–20

He who believes in the Son has eternal life. He who does not believe the Son shall not see life, but the wrath of God remains on him.

—John 3:36

That if you confess with your mouth Jesus is Lord, and believe in your heart that God has raised Him from the dead, you will be saved, for with the heart one believes unto righteousness, and with the mouth confession is made unto salvation.

—Romans 10:9–10

But sanctify the Lord God in your hearts. Always be ready to give an answer to every man who asks you for a reason for the hope that is in you, with gentleness and fear.

—1 Peter 3:15

In this is love: not that we loved God, but that He loved us and sent His Son to be the atoning sacrifice for our sins.

—1 John 4:10

WORK

The Lord will open up to you His good treasure, the heavens, to give the rain to your land in its season and to bless all the work of your hand. You will lend to many nations, but you will not borrow.

—Deuteronomy 28:12

But you all must be strong and not lose heart, for there is a reward for your deeds.

—2 Chronicles 15:7

Let the beauty of the Lord our God be upon us, and establish the work of our hands among us; yes, establish the work of our hands.

—Psalm 90:17

Let him who steals steal no more. Instead, let him labor, working with his hands things which are good, that he may have something to share with him who is in need.

—Ephesians 4:28

And whatever you do, do it heartily, as for the Lord and not for men, knowing that from the Lord you will receive the reward of the inheritance. For you serve the Lord Christ.

—Colossians 3:23–24

WORRY

You are my hiding place; You will preserve me from trouble; You will surround me with shouts of deliverance. Selah.

—Psalm 32:7

God is our refuge and strength, a well-proven help in trouble. Therefore we will not fear, though the earth be removed, and though the mountains be carried into the midst of the sea; though its waters roar and foam, though the mountains shake with its swelling. Selah

—Psalm 46:1–3

We are troubled on every side, yet not distressed; we are perplexed, but not in despair; persecuted, but not forsaken; cast down, but not destroyed.

—2 Corinthians 4:8–9

But my God shall supply your every need according to His riches in glory by Christ Jesus.

—Philippians 4:19

But let him ask in faith, without wavering. For he who wavers is like a wave of the sea, driven and tossed with the wind.

—James 1:6

WORSHIP

Give to the Lord the glory of His name; worship the Lord in holy splendor.

—Psalm 29:2

O sing unto the Lord a new song; sing unto the Lord, all the earth!…For the Lord is great, and greatly to be praised; He is to be feared above all gods....Honor and majesty are before Him; strength and beauty are in His sanctuary.

—Psalm 96:1–6

Give unto the Lord the glory due His name; bring an offering, and come into His courts. Worship the Lord in the beauty of holiness; tremble before Him, all the earth. Say among the nations, "The Lord reigns! Indeed, the world is established; it shall not be moved; He shall judge the peoples righteously."

—Psalm 96:8–11

Exalt the Lord our God, and worship at His holy mountain; for the Lord our God is holy!

—Psalm 99:9

Enter into His gates with thanksgiving, and into His courts with praise; be thankful to Him, and bless His name.

—Psalm 100:4

STAND STRONG ON GOD'S PROMISE

*Transform your mind, heart, and soul through
the power of God's Word, and live with joy.*

978-1-62136-566-2 | US $4.99   978-1-62136-578-5 | US $4.99   978-1-62136-610-2 | US $4.99

MODERN
ENGLISH
VERSION

The SpiritLed Promises series makes it easy for you
to find the perfect verse for whatever situation you face.

The MEV Bible is the most modern translation in the King James tradition.
This version accurately communicates God's Word in a way
that combines the beauty of the past with clarity for today.

12930   **AVAILABLE AT BOOKSTORES EVERYWHERE**

Facebook.com/PassioFaith Twitter.com/PassioFaith www.PassioFaith.com   PASSIO
THE ART OF AUTHENTIC FAITH

Continue Pursing a Passionate Life in the Spirit

with these FREE Newsletters

New Man
Get articles about the realities of living in today's world as a man of faith.

SpiritLed Woman
Get amazing stories, testimonies and articles on marriage, family, prayer, and more.

Charisma Magazine
Get top-trending articles, Christian teachings, entertainment reviews, videos, and more.

The Ministry Today Report
Stay informed with practical commentary, news, and articles for pastors and leaders.

Be

EMPOWERED
INSPIRED
ENCOURAGED
PASSIONATE

SIGN UP AT:
nl.charismamag.com

CHARISMA MEDIA